Top 25 locator map
(continues on inside
back cover)
◄

KU-391-011

CityPack
London

LOUISE NICHOLSON

If you have any comments or
suggestions for this guide you
can contact the editor at
Citypack@the AA.com

AA Publishing
Find out more about AA Publishing and the wide range
of travel publications and services the AA provides by
visiting our web site at *www.theAA.com/bookshop*

About this Book

KEY TO SYMBOLS

🔟 Map reference to the accompanying fold-out map, and Top 25 locator map

✉ Address

☎ Telephone number

🕐 Opening/closing times

🍴 Restaurant or café on premises or nearby

🚇 Nearest Tube (formerly known as the Underground) station

🚊 Nearest railway station

🚌 Nearest bus route

🚤 Nearest riverboat or ferry stop

♿ Facilities for visitors with disabilities

✋ Admission charges: Expensive (over £6), Moderate (£3–6) and Inexpensive (under £3)

↔ Other nearby places of interest

❓ Other practical information

➤ Indicates the page where you will find a fuller description

ℹ Tourist information

ORGANIZATION

This guide is divided into six sections:

- Planning Ahead and Getting There
- Living London—London Now, London Then, Time to Shop, Out and About, Walks, London by Night
- London's Top 25 Sights
- London's Best—best of the rest
- Where to—detailed listings of restaurants, hotels, shops and nightlife
- Travel facts—packed with practical information

In addition, easy-to-read side panels provide extra facts and snippets, highlights of places to visit and invaluable practical advice.

The colours of the tabs on the page corners match the colours of the triangles aligned with the chapter names on the contents page opposite.

MAPS

The fold-out map in the wallet at the back of the book is a comprehensive street plan of London. The first (or only) map reference given for each attraction refers to this map. **The Top 25 locator maps** found on the inside front and back covers of the book itself are for quick reference. They show the Top 25 Sights, described on pages 26–50, which are clearly plotted by number (**1**–**25**, not page number) across the city. The second map reference given for the Top 25 Sights refers to this map.

Contents

Planning Ahead

WHEN TO GO

The tourist season is year round, and almost all attractions remain open throughout the year. The peak season is between June and September, when you should arrive with a hotel reservation and theatre tickets. The quietest months are November, January and February, when you may find discounts on hotel rooms.

TIME

GMT (Greenwich Mean Time) is standard. BST (British Summer Time) is 1 hour ahead (late Mar–late Oct).

AVERAGE DAILY TEMPERATURE

JAN	FEB	MAR	APR	MAY	JUN	JUL	AUG	SEP	OCT	NOV	DEC
42°F	45°F	50°F	55°F	63°F	68°F	72°F	72°F	66°F	57°F	50°F	45°F
6°C	7°C	10°C	13°C	17°C	20°C	22°C	22°C	19°C	14°C	10°C	7°C

Spring (March to May) has a mixture of sunshine and showers, although winter often encroaches on it.

Summer (June to August) can be unpredictable, with clear skies and searing heat one day followed by sultry greyness and thunderstorms the next.

Autumn (September to November) has clear skies that can feel almost summery. Real autumn starts in October, and colder weather sets in during November.

Winter (December to February) is generally mild, with the odd cold snap, and snow is uncommon.

WHAT'S ON

January *Sales*: Shopping bargains at stores all over the city.

February *Chinese New Year*: Dragon dances and fireworks in Soho.

March *Chelsea Antiques Fair*: Chelsea Old Town Hall.

April *Oxford and Cambridge Boat Race* (1st Sat): Putney to Mortlake on the Thames.

London Marathon (1st Sun): The world's biggest running race..

May *Chelsea Flower Show* (end of May): One of the world's best, at the Royal Hospital, Chelsea.

June *Trooping the Colour* (2nd Sat): The 'Colours' (flags) are trooped before the Queen on Horseguards Parade, Whitehall.

Wimbledon (Jun/Jul): The world's leading grass tennis tournament.

July *Promenade Concerts* (Jul–Aug): Nightly world-class classical concerts in the Albert Hall.

August *Notting Hill Carnival* (last weekend, Bank Holiday Monday): Europe's biggest carnival.

September *Election of the Lord Mayor of London* (29 Sep): The Lord Mayor and his successor-elect ride in the state coach to the Mansion House.

October *Pearly Kings and Queens* (1st Sun): Service at St. Martin's-in-the-Fields.

November *Bonfire Night* (5 Nov): Fires and fireworks commemorate the failed Gunpowder Plot of 1605.

State Opening of Parliament: Royal procession from Buckingham Palace to the Houses of Parliament.

December *Christmas music* (all month): Christmas music fills London's churches.

LONDON ONLINE

www.londontown.com
London's official site is up to date and comprehensive with ideas for museums, theatre and restaurants, and sections for children and visitors with disabilities. It offers discounts, too.

www.london-tourist-information.com
A lively website with everything from travel tips to a reservation service, plus useful links to other London-related sites.

www.londontransport.co.uk
London Transport's official site gives ideas for what to see and do, plus ticket information for the Tube, buses, DLR and river services. It also has a WAP-enabled journey planner.

www.royal.gov.uk
The official site of the British royal family, with history, royal residences, who's doing what today and a monthly online magazine.

www.bhrc.co.uk
The British Hotel Reservation Centre website takes bookings, from bed-and-breakfasts to grand hotels. Includes special discounts.

www.londonpass.com
On this site you can buy the London Pass card valid for 3 or 6 days, with unlimited access to over 50 London attractions and public transport.

www.londonpagesonline.com
Chatty website covering London's well-known attractions plus some of the less known.

www.hrp.org.uk
London's five great historic palaces, from the Tower of London to Hampton Court.

www.officiallondontheatre.com
The Society of London Theatre's official site, with all the latest theatre news plus comprehensive interviews with stars, performance details and theatre access for people with disabilities.

GOOD TRAVEL SITES

www.nationaltrust.org.uk
This independent organization owns and maintains many buildings and extensive lands, some of them in and around London.

www.english-heritage.org.uk/London
English Heritage are responsible for many historic sites and buildings—many are in London.

www.fodors.com
A complete travel-planning site. You can research prices and weather; book air tickets, cars and rooms; pose questions (and get answers) from fellow travellers; and find links to other sites.

CYBERCAFÉS
easyInternetcafé (easyEverything.com):
The international chain started in London is open seven days a week and has branches throughout the city. The one at 160–166 Kensington High Street has almost 400 terminals

Getting There

VISAS AND TRAVEL INSURANCE

Visas are not required for EU, US or Canadian nationals, but you will need a valid passport. EU citizens are covered for medical expenses with form E111. However, insurance to cover illness and theft is still strongly advised. Visitors from outside the EU should check their insurance coverage before travelling and if necessary, buy a supplementary policy.

MONEY

Try to arrive at the airport or railway station with some British coins, or a £10 or £5 note. If you travel to your hotel by Underground, the self-service machines accept coins and low value notes (bills).

£5

£10

£20

ARRIVING

Heathrow and Gatwick are the principal airports serving the city. However, Stansted, Luton and London City are becoming increasingly busy with traffic from continental Europe. There are train links to the continent via Lille and Paris and road links to Channel ports.

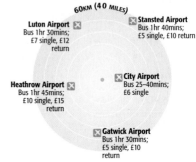

60KM (40 MILES)

Luton Airport 🗙
Bus 1hr 30mins;
£7 single, £12
return

🗙 **Stansted Airport**
Bus 1hr 40mins;
£5 single, £10 return

Heathrow Airport 🗙
Bus 1hr 45mins;
£10 single, £15
return

🗙 **City Airport**
Bus 25–40mins;
£6 single

🗙 **Gatwick Airport**
Bus 1hr 30mins;
£5 single, £10
return

FROM HEATHROW

Heathrow (☎ 0870 000 0123) has four terminals 24km (15 miles) west of central London; all are well served by public transport. On the Tube (formerly know as the Underground) the Piccadilly line runs from 5am–midnight (6am–1pm on Sunday); the trip takes around an hour. The Heathrow Express (☎ 0845 600 1515), a high-speed rail link to Paddington station, runs from 5.10am–midnight. Ticket prices are high for the 15-minute journey. National Express (0870 580 8080) buses run 5.30am–9.30pm but the trip can take more than an hour. Taxis can be picked up outside any terminal; the trip takes about one hour–dependent on the traffic; cost around £60.

FROM GATWICK

Gatwick airport (☎ 0870 000 2468) is 48km (30 miles) south of the heart of the city. The best way to reach London is by train: The Gatwick Express (0845 850 1530) train leaves Victoria Station every 15 minutes, (5am–1am) and takes 30 minutes. Connex runs slightly slower but cheaper services; and Thameslink leads direct to the City and King's Cross. Taxis cost more than £100.

From Stansted

Stansted airport (☎ 0870 000 0303) is 56km (35 miles) northeast of central London. The Stansted Express (☎ 0845 748 950) takes around 40 minutes. Airbus A6 (☎ 0870 580 8080) runs 24 hours and takes up to 1 hour 40 minutes. A taxi costs around £100.

From Luton Airport

Luton airport (☎ 01582 405 100) is 53km (33 miles) north of London. There are bus links to Victoria Coach Station, taking around 1 hour 30 minutes and Thameslink trains to King's Cross, which take 40 minutes. Taxis cost about £80.

From London City Airport

City Airport (☎ 020 7646 0000) is at Royal Albert Docks, the Docklands, 9 miles (14km) east of central London. The Airport Shuttle Bus runs to Liverpool Street station; bus 473 connects to the DLR (Docklands Light Railway) station Prince Regent. Taxis wait outside the terminal and cost around £24.

From the Channel Tunnel

Eurostar (☎ 0870 160 6600; www.eurostar.com) arrives in Waterloo Station, where you can catch a bus, the Tube, or a taxi. Eurotunnel (☎ www. eurotunnel.com) is for vehicles only. No reservations are necessary, but fares are lower if you've reserved ahead. They run three times an hour daily between Calais and Folkestone where you can join the M20 to London.

Getting Around (also ► 91–92)

Buses and Tube trains run from around 5.30am to just after midnight, when service is via a night bus. The transport system is divided into zones—six for the Tube and four for buses—and you must have a ticket valid for the zone you are in. If you anticipate more than one journey, buy a travelcard, which allows unlimited use of the Tube, buses and train services in the London area after 9.30am. Other discounts are available (► 91). Taxis that are available illuminate a yellow 'For Hire' sign on the roof. Hold out your hand to hail them.

DRIVING TIP

Driving in London is slow, parking is expensive and fines are high—use public transport. Congestion charges operate from Monday to Friday, 7am–6.30pm, costing £5 a day.

VISITORS WITH DISABILITIES

London is steadily improving its facilities for visitors with disabilities, from shops and theatres to hotels and museums. The Government is introducing free admission for those with disabilities. Newer attractions such as Tate Modern and the London Eye are better equipped than ancient buildings such as Westminster Abbey. Check out the London Tourist Board's comprehensive website www.londontouristboard. com and guidebooks, such as *Accessible Britain*, covering accommodation (published annually by the English Tourism Council) and *The Museum's Guide* (published by Artsline).

William Forrester, a lecturer and wheelchair user, leads tailor-made tours in the city (☎ 01483 575401).

Living
London

London Now

Above: *You'll get a bird's-eye view across London from the British Airways London Eye*
Right: *From power station to state of the art—Tate Modern*

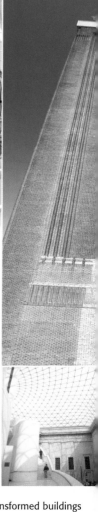

TAKING TEA

• The immobilizing ritual of afternoon tea—cucumber sandwiches, scones (biscuits) and cream, little cakes and pots of Darjeeing tea—is best enjoyed in a grand hotel such as The Dorchester, Claridge's and the Mandarin Oriental Hyde Park.

Few cities celebrated the new millennium with as much verve as London. Known for its pomp, pageantry and colourful history, the dawn of the year 2000 saw the British capital looking forward rather than back. The regeneration of the Thames' riverbanks and the completion of major public projects were then the settings for further celebrations during the Queen's Golden Jubilee throughout 2002.

Whole areas of the capital have been revitalized. London's new additions range from imaginatively transformed buildings to dramatic fresh architecture, epitomized by Tate Modern (► 47) and the British Airways London Eye (► 42). The first is a brilliant example of renovation, the second a masterpiece of

Above: *Café scene in Covent Garden*
Left: *Harley Davidson on the King's Road*

CAFÉ SOCIETY

• Twenty years ago, the idea of sitting at a pavement café and sipping a coffee or a beer was considered a Continental habit. Londoners ate and drank indoors. Today, however, they think nothing of lingering at outside tables, chatting over an espresso or a cappuchino. In winter, heaters and windbreaks allow the alfresco café society to continue on sunny days. Even the traditionally dark and smoke-filled pubs have spread beyond their doors. In fine weather, pavements can look like obstacle courses; why not sit down and enjoy the passing parade?

LONDON WALKS

• Guided walks cater for most interests. Learn about haunted pubs, Charles Dickens or the Old Jewish East End. Join a Beatles Magical Mystery Tour; discover saucy Southwark on a Prisons, Pilgrims, Prostitutes and Players walk. Check listings in *Time Out*. See also ► 20, 22–23).

Above: *Diplodocus in the cathedral-like Natural History Museum*
Above right: *The Imax Cinema on the South Bank*
Right: *Entrance to the Earth Galleries, Natural History Museum*

engineering technology, but both capture the public's imagination in very different ways.

Tate Modern, a vast, outdated power station on the depressed south bank of the Thames, is now home to the national collection of modern art. By contrast, the London Eye is pure fun. Dominating the sky above the River Thames, this ultra-modern wheel stands diagonally across from the Big Ben tower. Tate Modern and the Eye sandwich the South Bank

A TRULY COSMOPOLITAN CITY

• Londoners have brought a rich mixture of cultures and traditions to the city over the past 2,000 years. With its great port, London has been an international city of immigrants since Roman times. And people still arrive from all over the world to live and work there. Now, as part of the European Union, you will find French and Italians working in restaurants and cafés, Swedish and Dutch selling clothes in shops, and Belgians and Spanish greeting you at hotel reception desks. You'll find many Antipodeans in the bars, too.

arts complex galvanizing the long-term regeneration of the Thames' riverside, stretching 3.5km (2 miles) to Tower Bridge and beyond. Here there is much to explore: Shakespeare's Globe Theatre, the BFI Imax cinema, the National Theatre, the Millennium Bridge, and plenty of lively cafés.

Above: *Neal's Yard in Covent Garden—the alternative place for health foods and natural remedies*

LONDONERS HAVE THEIR SAY

• You won't necessarily find Londoners agreeing. They love to complain about everything from the weather to schools, congestion charges in the city and health issues. While visitors praise the efficiency of the public transport system, Londoners remember when it was better. After the Greater London Council was abolished in 1983 Londoners had no voice and no authority to whom they could complain. When the new GLA, Greater London Authority, was founded in 1999, Londoners elected their first mayor of all London in the city's history. The issues faced are the same as other major cities: public transport, affordable housing and the environment. With a central London population of 7.5 million, some 250,000 businesses and 28 million visitors a year these issues can't be taken lightly.

ON THE BALL

• London has more competitive soccer teams than any other city. Arsenal, Chelsea, Fulham and Tottenham Hotspur are the most famous, and weekend tickets are hard to get. Try mid-week, or watch one of the other pro clubs. The soccer season runs from August until May.

Above: *Inside Canary Wharf*
Right: *Carnival time at Notting Hill*
Above right: *Cooling off in Trafalgar Square*

Elsewhere in the capital, performance arts have benefited from the completion of major rebuilding projects at the Royal Opera House and Sadler's Wells Theatre. Even more intriguing are three ingenious roofing projects for museums: over the inner courtyard of the British Museum, creating a visitor-friendly Great Court; over the internal courtyard of the Wallace Collection (► 53); and over the new galleries at the National Maritime Museum. Meanwhile, Somerset House, once a palatial riverside office for civil servants, is home to a clutch of museums. Its courtyard, once used for parking cars, is now a relaxing place to enjoy summer fountains and winter ice-skating.

Beneath the ground, the extension to the Jubilee Underground line is another success. It runs from Westminster eastwards along the South Bank in the City and East End. Not only does it provide new links but each of the ten stations was individually designed by leading architects

including Sir Norman Foster (Canary Wharf) and Will Alsopp (North Greenwich), creating bright, clean exciting new spaces.

Above ground, new measures to control pollution and traffic problems have been brought in. The Mayor of London, Ken Livingstone, has introduced a congestion charge in the heart of the city, which operates Monday to Friday from 7am until 6.30pm in an effort to reduce the traffic.

Not all the millennium projects were successful. The gigantic Millennium Dome in Greenwich was universally condemned; despite attracting some 6 million visitors in its opening year, the interior displays were sold off and the building closed. Its future remains uncertain.

Overall, however, the effect of new millennium projects was positive and the Jubilee celebrations were taken to the hearts of the people. The buzz and the excitement recalls the 1960s when London led the world in design and creativity. British fashion designers, musicians, architects and artists are making waves wherever they go: London is hot once again.

SIR CHRISTOPHER WREN

● In the jumble of styles that make up London's cityscape, one architect's legacy dominates. Sir Christopher Wren (1632–1723) designed St. Paul's Cathedral and 51 churches, whose soaring spires have inspired builders across the world. Classic Wren churches include St. Mary-le-Bow and St. Bride's in Fleet Street.

15

London Then

Above: *The Tower of London from an engraving of 1597*

BEFORE 1000

Emperor Claudius invades Britain in AD43; a deep-water port, Londinium, is soon established.

In the year 200 the Romans put a wall around Londinium, now capital of Britannia Superior; they withdrew in 410.

THE GREAT FIRE

The fire broke out at a baker's near Pudding Lane on the night of 2 September 1666. Raging for four days and nights, it destroyed four-fifths of the City of London and 13,200 homes. Sir Christopher Wren became the grand architect of the consequent rebuilding of London.

1042 Edward the Confessor becomes king making London capital of England and Westminster his home; begins the abbey church of St. Peter.

1066 The Norman king, William the Conqueror, defeats King Harold at the Battle of Hastings; begins the Tower of London.

1485 Tudor rule begins, ending in 1603 with the death of Elizabeth I.

1533 Henry VIII breaks with Rome to marry Anne Boleyn; establishes the Church of England.

1649 Charles I is executed in Whitehall; the Commonwealth (1649–53) and Protectorate (1653–59) govern England until Charles II is restored to the throne in 1660.

1666 The Great Fire of London.

1759 The British Museum, London's first public museum opens.

1851 The Great Exhibition is held in Hyde Park.

1863 World's first urban underground train service opens. In 1890 the first deep-dug train runs (known as 'the Tube').

1939–45 Blitz bombings destroy a third of the City of London and much of the docks.

1951 Festival of Britain held on the site of the South Bank arts complex.

1960s The Beatles, Carnaby Street and the King's Road help create 'swinging London'.

1980s Post-war conservation movements save 30,000 London buildings from demolition.

1981 Revival of Docklands begins.

1994 First Eurostar trains link London and Paris through Channel Tunnel.

2000 Major millennium projects are completed, rejuvenating central London.

2002 Queen Elizabeth II celebrates her Golden Jubilee. City Hall completed for the Mayor of London.

2003 Clarence House, formerly the Queen Mother's home, opens to the public. Fiftieth anniversary of Queen Elizabeth II's accession to the throne.

2004 30 St Mary Axe, designed by Foster and Partners, wins the RIBA Sterling Prize for architecture.

From second left: *The Great Fire of London, 1666, from a painting by Lieve Verschuier; the celebrated Festival of Britain, 1951; the 'Swinging Sixties' with fashion model Twiggy and friends*

GROWING CITY

During the 16th century, London was Europe's fastest-growing city; its population rose from 75,000 to 200,000.

By 1700, London was Europe's biggest and wealthiest city, with about 700,000 people.

London continued to grow, from under 1 million in 1800 to 6.5 million by 1900, peaking in the 1930s and 1940s at 10 million.

The population is now 7.5 million but rising.

Time to Shop

BEST OF BRITISH

Take home some British souvenirs with a difference. You can buy beautifully crafted umbrellas and walking sticks from James Smith & Sons (✉ 53 New Oxford Street, WC1). For a good British cheese buy a Stilton, all ready and packed, from Paxton & Whitfield (✉ 93 Jermyn Street, SW1). If you want to try some British recipes go to Books for Cooks (✉ 4 Blenheim Crescent, W11) for a large selection of cookbooks. Tea addicts should head for The Tea House (✉ 15A Neale Street, WC2) for a choice of blends and some stylish teapots. English herbs, oils and toiletries from Culpeper Herbalists (✉ 8 The Market, WC2) make great presents.

If England really is a nation of shopkeepers, then London is the head office. You can hunt down almost anything if you are determined enough. Britain's unique position between Europe and the Americas, bolstered by its colonial connections to Africa, Asia and Australasia, ensures that saris and spices are as easy to find as Vegemite and rare reggae records. For shoppers, the choice ranges from vibrant street markets to legendary department stores and from off-beat boutiques to smart galleries of paintings and antiques.

It is the range that excites visitors, whether in antiques, classics or cutting-edge contemporary. London has outrageous fashion, bolstered by the annual crop of imaginative art, fashion and design school graduates. By contrast, long-established shopping streets, such as Oxford Street and Kensington High Street, offer mass-market goods, while markets such as Camden Lock and Portobello Road (see main picture above) are eclectic, ethnic and inexpensive.

London's souvenirs range from tatty to tasteful. Ever since the Swinging Sixties, anything with a Union Jack flag on it has sold well, from T-shirts to garish hats. For high quality, go to museums' in-house shops. Gifts at the shop in Buckingham Palace Mews include the Queen Victoria range

Something for everyone—shopping in London can be hip or refreshingly traditional. From cobbled markets to Regency arcades—London is the place to shop

of china, a mini throne for a charm bracelet or a guardsman puppet. The Victoria and Albert Museum, British Museum and National Gallery also stock quality items inspired by their diverse collections—you can do a full-scale Christmas shop at any of these. The Design Museum offers immensely chic designer goods—some with very high price tags—while the Museum of London is particularly good for souvenirs and books about London. At the National Portrait Gallery, with its two large shops, you will find books on historical figures and British history, as well as a good supply of postcards and posters.

Go to St. James's or Knightsbridge for traditional British-made goods such as tweed jackets, flat caps and handmade shoes or delicate fragrances, elegant china, floral printed fabrics and, of course, cashmere sweaters. London still has long-established businesses with world-wide reputations. Visit Burlington Arcade (see main picture above) for its specialist up-market shops in an historic setting. Burberry and Aquascutum are synonymous with raincoats. Harrods has been trading for some 150 years; Selfridges was the country's first department store; and Liberty fabrics are still exotic and luxurious. Their January and July sales are major events on any shoppers' calendar.

SHOP THE SHOP

Charles Dickens would recognize many London shops. Burlington Arcade, off Piccadilly, is a 18th-century covered shopping mall, with a liveried beadle to maintain decorum. Many shops display the royal insignia, showing that they supply members of the royal household with everything from brushes to jewels (www.royalwarrant.org). For instance, John Lobb (✉ 9 St. James's Street, SW1) custom makes shoes and boots for the royal family—and for you, at a price.

Out & About

Above: *The* Cutty Sark
moored at Greenwich

INFORMATION

GREENWICH
Distance 6km (4 miles)
from London Bridge and
Tower Hill, 8km (5 miles)
from Westminster Bridge
Journey time 20
minutes–1 hour
🚈 Docklands Light
Railway to Island Gardens,
then foot tunnel, or
continue to Cutty Sark
Station
🚢 Riverboat from
Westminster and other
piers
🏠 Pepys House, 2 Cutty
Sark Gardens, SE10
☎ 0870 608 2000
🕐 Daily 10–5

NATIONAL MARITIME
MUSEUM
✉ Romney Road, SE10
☎ 020 8858 4422
🕐 Daily 10–5 (Jul and
Aug until 6)
🎫 Free

ORGANIZED SIGHTSEEING

A guided tour is a good way to gain in-depth information from a Londoner. Walking tours get into London life. They have good leaders, cost little and do not require advance booking. Try the Original London Walks (☎ 020 7624 3978). Bus tours have various pick-up points, including some hotels. Try the Big Bus Company, with live commentary on double-decker buses (☎ 0800 169 1365) or go for a tailor-made tour with a highly trained Blue Badge guide (☎ 020 7495 5504).

EXCURSIONS
GREENWICH

Six kilometres (4 miles) downstream from the City lies Greenwich. At its core is a favourite royal palace, the Queen's House, designed by Inigo Jones in 1616, which is surrounded by Christopher Wren's buildings for the Royal Naval Hospital. Go early and for the whole day. There is plenty to see, plus markets and craft fairs at weekends (➤ 74).

The National Maritime Museum, the world's largest nautical museum, fills the old Royal Hospital School, incorporates Queen's House, and has state of the art galleries opened in 2000. Up the hill is the Royal Observatory, Greenwich—the Greenwich Meridian (0° longitude) passes through here. Nearby, the park's broad terrace provides London's grandest view; behind lie the Ranger's House and the Fan Museum. Also check out the Painted Hall and Chapel inside Wren's Hospital, and two special boats: the *Cutty Sark* built in 1869, and Sir Francis Chichester's yacht *Gipsy Moth IV* in which he undertook his solo round-the-world voyage in 1966–67.

Middle: *Hampton Court Palace—fit for a king or queen*
Left: *The regal splendour of Windsor Castle dominates the River Thames*

HAMPTON COURT PALACE

This is London's most impressive royal palace, well worth the journey west out of the city. When King Henry VIII dismissed Cardinal Wolsey in 1529, he took over his already ostentatious Tudor palace and enlarged it. Successive monarchs altered and repaired both the palace and its 12ha (29 acres) of Tudor and baroque gardens.

The best way to visit this huge collection of chambers, courtyards and state apartments is to follow one of the six clearly indicated routes—perhaps Henry VIII's State Apartments or the King's Apartments built for William III, immaculately restored after a devastating fire. Outside, do not miss the Tudor gardens, the Maze and restored Privy Garden, where there are guided historical walks each afternoon.

WINDSOR

The fairy-tale towers and turrets of Windsor Castle make this official residence of the Queen the ultimate queen's castle. Begun by William the Conqueror, rebuilt in stone by Henry II, it has been embellished periodically. Various parts are open; if the State Apartments and St. George's Chapel are closed, there is still plenty to see. Don't miss Queen Mary's Dolls' House designed by Edward Lutyens. Changing of the Guard is at 11am.

Outside the castle lie Windsor's pretty, medieval cobblestone lanes, Christopher Wren's Guildhall and the delightful Theatre Royal. Beyond it, you can explore 1,950-ha (4,700-acre) Windsor Great Park, cross the Thames to Eton or visit Legoland.

INFORMATION

HAMPTON COURT
Distance 18km (11 miles)
Journey time 30 minutes by train, 3–4 hours by boat
🚆 Waterloo railway station to Hampton Court
🚢 Riverboat from Westminster Pier

HAMPTON COURT PALACE
✉ East Molesey, Surrey
☎ 0870 752 7777
🕐 Apr–end Oct Tue–Sun 9.30–6 (also Mon 10.15–6); Nov–end Mar Tue–Sun 9.30–4.30 (also Mon 10.15–4.30)
💷 Expensive

WINDSOR
Distance 28km (17 miles)
Journey time 35–50 minutes
🚆 Waterloo or Paddington
ℹ 24 High Street
☎ 01753 743900
🕐 Daily 10–5

WINDSOR CASTLE
☎ 01753 831118
🕐 Mar–end Oct daily 9.45–5; Nov–end Feb 9.45–4
💷 Expensive

Walks

INFORMATION

Distance Approx 2.5km
(1½ miles)
Time 2–3 hours,
depending on indoor
visits
Start point ★
Tower Bridge
⊞ K6
Ⓜ Tower Hill
End point Royal Festival
Hall, South Bank
⊞ G6
Ⓜ Waterloo
🚆 Waterloo

THE SOUTH BANK: THE DESIGN MUSEUM TO WESTMINSTER BRIDGE

This walk hugs the riverbank and enjoys superb views across London's core. Begin at Tower Bridge Museum for high-level views, then stroll eastwards among the old warehouses and new restaurants of Shad Thames to find Anthony Donaldson's *Waterfall* sculpture in Tower Bridge Piazza, Eduardo Paolozzi's riverside sculpture and the riverfront Design Museum on Butler's Wharf.

West of Tower Bridge, past shimmering City Hall, the path leads to HMS *Belfast* and Hay's Galleria for more cafés. Outside the Cottons Centre is a pavilion where a map plots the buildings along the City view. Over London Bridge take in Southwark Cathedral (worth going inside) and, after the Golden Hinde replica galleon, a wall and rose window of the 14th-century Winchester Palace's Great Hall.

Between Southwark and Blackfriars bridges are Shakespeare's Globe Theatre, Tate Modern and the Oxo Tower. The riverfront widens at the South Bank arts complex; the BA London Eye, Saatchi Gallery and London Aquarium lie beyond. Take Hungerford footbridge for Charing Cross, Westminster Bridge for Westminster.

0 ½ km
0 ½ mile

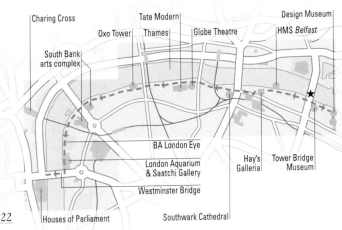

Charing Cross | Tate Modern | Design Museum
Oxo Tower | Thames | Globe Theatre | HMS *Belfast*
South Bank arts complex
BA London Eye
London Aquarium & Saatchi Gallery | Hay's Galleria | Tower Bridge Museum
Westminster Bridge
Houses of Parliament | Southwark Cathedral

THE TWO CITIES: CITY OF WESTMINSTER TO THE CITY OF LONDON

The heart of Westminster is still Westminster Abbey and the Houses of Parliament—there is a good view of the riverfront from the south end of Westminster Bridge.

From statue-filled Parliament Square, Whitehall leads up past Downing Street, Horse Guards and Banqueting House, to Trafalgar Square, home of the National Gallery. Turn up St. Martin's Lane, passing the National Portrait Gallery. Farther up this street, past the Coliseum, turn right through New Row into Covent Garden—good for refreshments. On the piazza, find the London Transport Museum and nearby, the Theatre Museum. Down on the Strand, turn left and find Somerset House's museums at Aldwych.

In Fleet Street, a winged dragon marks the boundary of the City of London and Westminster. Just before Chancery Lane, an alley on the right leads to Temple Church and the Inner and Middle Inns. Farther on, Johnson's Court (between Nos. 166 and 167), leads to Dr. Johnson's House. St. Paul's Cathedral stands at the top of Ludgate Hill. Behind it, Watling Street leads to Bow Lane and a choice of restaurants.

INFORMATION

Distance 3.5km (2–2½ miles)
Time 3–6 hours, depending on museum and church visits
Start point ★
Westminster Bridge
⊞ G6
🚇 Westminster
End point Bow Street
⊞ G5
🚇 Mansion House

0   ½ km

Dr. Johnson's House

Fleet Street

River Thames

St. Paul's Cathedral

Theatre Museum
London Transport Museum
Aldwych
Covent Garden
Coliseum
National Portrait Gallery
National Gallery
Trafalgar Square
Banqueting House
Downing Street
Bow Lane
Parliament Square
Westminster Abbey
Temple Church
Inns of Court
Houses of Parliament
Westminster Bridge
Somerset House

London by Night

Above: If the weather permits join the pavement party in Soho

Above right: Theatreland— Shaftesbury Avenue

London changes with the seasons, especially after dark. In the depths of winter, dusk falls at 4.30 in the afternoon; in summer it stays light until 10pm. The fogs that added atmosphere to Alfred Hitchcock's films are long gone, but winters can be damp, so Londoners walk with energy and purpose, rather than at a leisurely pace. Perhaps this explains the popularity of London's traditional pubs and modern bars: Even Londoners need to go indoors and warm up. Guided after-dark walks to historic and haunted pubs are an ideal way to explore the city in autumn and winter.

Come summer, London's outdoors comes into its own. Londoners enjoy concerts in settings such as Hampton Court Palace, Kenwood House, Hyde Park and Kew Gardens. The music ranges from classical and opera to jazz and rock 'n' roll. In elegant Kensington, the Holland Park Theatre puts on first-class opera and ballet against a backdrop of the remains of the 17th-century Holland House. The Regent's Park Open Air Theatre has mounted fine performances of Shakespeare for over 70 years. Sometimes there is covered seating; or spectators sit on the grass. Although there is usually food on sale, many Londoners prefer to picnic. It's part of the pleasure of summer in the city.

Year round the diversity of the club scene is legendary and with many changing themes weekly, check before you go. There are tried and tested venues for older clubbers and a host of new wave options (► 84) pulsing in the city.

WALK THE WALK

The 2-km (1-mile) long stretch of riverside between Westminster and London bridges bustles by night, as well as by day. The London Eye (open until 8pm, or later) is magical after dark. On the opposite bank, illuminated landmarks include the Houses of Parliament and Somerset House. At Oxo Tower Wharf, go to the top floor for a drink or a meal. There are few better views of London. Admire Tate Modern (open until 10pm Fridays and Saturdays) and the Globe. Rest your feet at a riverside pub.

LONDON's
top 25 sights

The sights are shown on the maps on the inside front cover and inside back cover, numbered **1**–**25** across the city

THE NATURAL HISTORY MUSEUM

Top Visitor Attraction
Holiday Which Magazine

Children and Senior Citizens Free

Royal Botanical Gardens, Kew

HIGHLIGHTS

- Arriving by riverboat
- Japanese Gateway and Pagoda
- Gallery walks, Palm House
- Temperate House
- Springtime woods and dells
- Oak Avenue to Queen Charlotte's Cottage

INFORMATION

www.kew.org

- Off fold-out map; Locator map off A3
- Kew Road, Kew
- 020 8940 1171
- Daily from 9.30am; closing time varies
- Restaurants and cafés
- Kew Garden
- Kew Bridge
- Excellent ■ Moderate
- Guided tours 11, 2 from Victoria Gate; orchid show Feb–Mar

The Princess of Wales Conservatory

Whether the trees are shrouded in winter mists, the azaleas are bursting with blossoms, or the lawns are dotted with summer picnickers reading Sunday newspapers, Kew Gardens never fail to work their magic.

Royal beginnings The 120-ha (300-acre) gardens, containing 44,000 different plants and many glorious greenhouses, make up the world's foremost botanical research centre. But it began modestly. George III's mother, Princess Augusta, planted 4ha (9 acres) around tiny Kew Palace in 1759, helped by gardener William Aiton and botanist Lord Bute. Architect Sir William Chambers built the Pagoda, Orangery, Ruined Arch and three temples. Later, George III enlarged the gardens to their present size and Sir Joseph Banks (head gardener 1772–1819), who had travelled with Captain Cook, planted them with specimens from all over the world.

Victorian order When the gardens were given to the nation in 1841, Sir William Hooker became director for 24 years. He founded the Department of Economic Botany, the museums, the Herbarium and the Library, while W. A. Nesfield laid out the lake, pond and the four great vistas: Pagoda Vista, Broad Walk, Holly Walk and Cedar Vista.

The greenhouses Chambers' Orangery is now a shop and restaurant. Decimus Burton designed the Palm House (1844–48) and Temperate House (1860–62, when it was the world's largest greenhouse), which preserves some plants that are extinct in their countries of origin. See too Waterlily House (1852) and the Princess of Wales Conservatory (1987). The exhibition, Evolution, tells the story of plants down the centuries.

Kensington Palace & Gardens

It gives King William III a human dimension that he suffered from asthma, a modern complaint, and so moved out of dank Whitehall Palace to a mansion in the clean air of tiny Kensington village.

The perfect location The year he became king, 1689, William and his wife Mary bought their mansion, perfectly positioned for London socializing and country living. They brought in Sir Christopher Wren and Nicholas Hawksmoor to remodel and enlarge the house, and moved in for Christmas.

A favourite royal home Despite the small rooms, George I introduced palatial grandeur with Colen Campbell's staircase and state rooms, elegantly decorated by William Kent. Meanwhile, Queen Anne added the Orangery (the architect was Nicholas Hawksmoor, the woodcarver Grinling Gibbons) and annexed a chunk of royal Hyde Park, a trick repeated by George II's wife, Queen Caroline, who created the Round Pond and Long Water to complete the 110-ha (275-acre) Kensington Gardens. Today, a wide variety of trees are the backdrop for sculptures (George Frampton's fairytale Peter Pan), monuments (Prince Albert), and contemporary exhibitions at the Serpentine Gallery.

A very special childhood On 24 May 1819, Queen Victoria was born here. She was baptized in the splendid Cupola Room, spent her childhood in rooms overlooking the gardens (now filled with Victoria memorabilia) and, on 20 June 1837, learned here she was to be queen. Later she opened her childhood home to the public. There is a permanent exhibition about Diana, Princess of Wales.

HIGHLIGHTS

- King's Grand Staircase
- Presence Chamber
- Wind dial in the King's Gallery
- King's Drawing Room
- Princess Victoria's dolls' house
- Round Pond
- Tea in the Orangery
- Walks
- Diana, Princess of Wales Exhibition
- Italian Gardens

INFORMATION

www.kensingtonpalace.org.uk

- C6; Locator map off A3
- Kensington Gardens, W8
- 020 7937 9561. Serpentine Gallery 020 7402 6075
- Mar–end Oct daily 10–5; Nov–end Feb 10–4. Serpentine Gallery daily 1–6
- Café, Orangery
- High Street Kensington or Queensway
- Few
- Expensive; family tickets. Serpentine gallery free
- Natural History Museum (➤ 28), Science Museum (➤ 29), V&A Museum (➤ 30)
- Guided tour every 30 minutes

27

Natural History Museum

INFORMATION

www.nhm.ac.uk

🔖 C7; Locator map A3

✉ Cromwell Road, SW7; also entrance on Exhibition Road

☎ 020 7942 5000

🕐 Mon–Sat 10–5.50, Sun 11–5.50

🍴 Meals, snacks, picnic areas

🚇 South Kensington

♿ Excellent 🆓 Free

↔ Science Museum (► 29), V&A Museum (► 30)

❓ Regular tours, lectures, films, workshops

Top: The entrance hall
Below: The East Wing

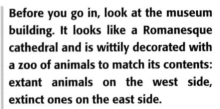

Before you go in, look at the museum building. It looks like a Romanesque cathedral and is wittily decorated with a zoo of animals to match its contents: extant animals on the west side, extinct ones on the east side.

Two museums in one Overflowing the British Museum, the Life Galleries were moved to Alfred Waterhouse's honey-and-blue-striped building in 1880. They tell the story of life on earth. The story of the earth itself is told in the Earth Galleries, beginning with a 300-million-year-old fossil of a fern. The Darwin Centre, uses IT to make the most of the museum's 70 million objects and the work of its 300 or so scientists accessible worldwide. A second phase due to open in 2007 will provide a much-needed new home for the museum's botany and entomology departments.

Dinosaurs in the Life Galleries The nave of Waterhouse's cathedral contains a plaster cast of the vast skeleton of the 150-million-year-old diplodocus (the original is in the US). Lively exhibition galleries focus on the relevance of the dinosaur world, the human body, mammals, birds, the marine world today and 'creepy crawlies' (the 800,000 known species of insect are added to every year)—all with plenty of models and hands-on games.

The Earth Galleries These offer a fascinating exploration of our planet, which includes the effects of natural forces on the earth such as earthquakes and the gemstones and minerals that lie beneath the earth's crust.

Science Museum

Even if you are no scientist, it's thrilling to understand how a plane flies, how Newton's reflecting telescope worked, or how we receive satellite television. You'll find answers using hands-on interactives. This is science made fun.

Industry and science   Opened in 1857 and once part of the Victoria & Albert Museum, this is the museum that comes closest to fulfilling Prince Albert's educational aims when he founded the South Kensington Museums after the Great Exhibition of 1851. Its full title is the National Museum of Science and Industry. Therefore, over the seven floors, which contain more than 60 collections, the story of human industry, discovery and invention is recounted through various tools and products, from exquisite Georgian cabinets to a satellite launcher.

Science made fun   People of all ages walk, talk, laugh and get excited by what they see here. You can see how vital every day objects were invented and then developed for use. The spinning wheel, steam engine, car and television have changed our lives. The industrial society in which we live could not do without plastic, but how is it made?

All kinds of science   The galleries vary from rooms of beautiful 18th-century objects to in-depth explanations of abstract concepts: You can use the hands-on equipment in Flight Lab to learn the basic principles of flying. The Wellcome Museum of the History of Medicine, on the topmost floors, includes an exhibit on prehistoric bone surgery and an X-ray room. The interactive Challenge of Materials and the high-tech Wellcome Wing explore science, technology and today's complex world.

HIGHLIGHTS

- Demonstrations
- Taking part in Launch Pad
- The hands-on basement area
- Flight Lab
- Apollo 10 module
- Puffing Billy
- Amy Johnson's aero-plane, *Jason*
- 18th-century watches and clocks
- The Wellcome Wing
- Historical characters explaining their achievements

INFORMATION

www.sciencemuseum.org.uk
- C7; Locator map A3
- Exhibition Road, SW7
- 020 7942 4455
- Daily 10–6
- Restaurants, cafés, picnic area in basement
- South Kensington
- Excellent, plus helpline
  020 7942 4446
- Free; Imax cinema expensive; Virtual Voyager moderate
- Guided tours, demonstrations, historic characters, lectures, films, workshops
- Natural History Museum (► 28)

Top: Apollo 10 module in the Exploration of Space Gallery

29

Victoria & Albert Museum

HIGHLIGHTS

- British Galleries
- Medieval ivory carvings
- The Jewellery Gallery
- Glass Gallery
- Whiteley Silver Galleries
- Canning Jewel
- Raphael Gallery
- Architecture Gallery
- The Hereford Screen

INFORMATION

www.vam.ac.uk
- D7; Locator map A3
- Cromwell Road, SW7
- 020 7942 2000; recorded information 0870 442 0808
- Daily 10–5.45 (Wed and last Fri open until 10pm)
- Restaurant, café
- South Kensington
- Very good   Free
- Natural History Museum (► 28), Science Museum (► 29)
- Guided tours, talks, courses, concerts

Detail, façade

Part of the Victoria & Albert Museum's glory is that each room is unexpected; it may contain a French boudoir, plaster casts of classical sculptures or exquisite contemporary glass, diverting you so happily that sometimes you will never reach your original goal.

An optimistic foundation   The V&A, as it is fondly known, started as the South Kensington Museum. It was Prince Albert's vision: Arts and science objects available to all people to inspire them to invent and create, with the accent on commercial design and craftsmanship. Since it opened in 1857, its collection has become so encyclopedic and international that today, it is the world's largest decorative arts museum.

Bigger and bigger   Its size is unmanageable: 11km (7 miles) of gallery space on six floors. Its content is even more so: Barely 5 per cent of the 44,000 objects in the Indian department can be on show. Larger museum objects include whole London house façades, grand rooms and the Raphael Cartoons. Despite this, contemporary work has always been energetically bought: More than 60 per cent of furniture entering the museum is 20th century.

Riches and rags   Not every object in the V&A is precious: There are everyday things, unique pieces and opportunities to discover a fascination for a new subject—perhaps lace, ironwork, tiles or Japanese textiles. The best way to tackle the V&A is either to select a favourite piece and go headlong for it, or wander happily for an hour or so, feasting on any objects that catch your eye. See the lavishly refurbished British Galleries, and the Whiteley Silver Galleries that show a magnificent collection of European silver.

Kenwood House & Hampstead Heath

For many north Londoners, sunny Sunday mornings on Hampstead Heath are an essential part of life: Locals walk their dogs and babies, sit reading the newspapers, enjoy the fine London views or drop into Kenwood House to see a Rembrandt or two.

Kenwood House   When in 1754 William Murray, Earl of Mansfield and George III's Chief Justice, bought his country house outside pretty Hampstead village spa, he brought in London's most fashionable architect, Robert Adam, to remodel it, and employed Humphry Repton to landscape the gardens. A later owner, Edward Guinness, Earl of Iveagh, hung the walls with Rembrandts, Gainsboroughs, Vermeers and Romneys before giving the whole package, the Iveagh Bequest, to the nation.

The people's heath   When Victorian London was expanding, it was the people of Hampstead who saved their valuable, open heathland from the developers' claws. Since 1829 they have preserved, piece by piece, a total of 335ha (825 acres) of rolling woodland, open grass and spectacular views—the walled Hill Garden was added only in 1960. It is 'to be kept forever…open, unenclosed and unbuilt on'.

A place of many moods   The heath is full of action and colour when weekend kite-flyers meet on Parliament Hill. It is a place for sports, perhaps swimming or boating in Hampstead Ponds, playing hockey on East Heath, enjoying a game of tennis or simply taking a quiet walk. There are arts celebrations, too, the best of which are the summer lakeside concerts that Londoners listen to as they picnic on the sloping lawns in front of Kenwood House.

HIGHLIGHTS

- Azaleas in the Hill Garden
- Library in Kenwood House
- Lakeside concerts
- London view from beside Kenwood House
- Oak, beech and sweet chestnut woods
- Parliament Hill
- Crossing the Heath from Hampstead to Highgate
- Rembrandt's *Portrait of the Artist* in Kenwood House
- Carpets of spring daffodils around Kenwood

INFORMATION

www.english-heritage.org.uk

➕ Off fold-out map; Locator map off A1

✉ Kenwood House, Hampstead Lane, NW3

☎ 020 8348 1286

🕐 Kenwood House Apr–end Sep daily 10–6; Oct 10–5, Nov–end Mar 10–4. The Heath daily 8am–dusk

🍴 Restaurant, café

🚇 Kenwood House: Golders Green. The Heath: Hampstead, Belsize Park, Highgate or Kentish Town

🚌 Kenwood House: 210

🚉 Gospel Oak, Hampstead Heath

♿ Good   💷 Free

❓ Guided tours for groups, outdoor concerts

Regent's Park

HIGHLIGHTS

- Queen Mary's Gardens
- Lakeside strolls
- Lolling on deckchairs by the bandstand
- Wildfowl Breeding Centre
- Boating on the lake
- London's central mosque
- Canal boat trip from the zoo to Little Venice
- Picnicking on the lake's north bank
- Summer barbecues at the open-air theatre

INFORMATION

➕ E3; Locator map B1
✉ Marylebone Road, NW1
☎ 020 7486 7905
🕐 Daily 7am to shortly before dusk (times are posted on information boards at each gate)
🍴 Restaurant, cafés
Ⓜ Marleybone, Baker Street, Regent's Park, Great Portland Street or Camden Town
♿ Very good
🔁 London Zoo (➤ 33), Madame Tussaud's Waxworks & Planetarium (➤ 61)
❓ Information boards at entrances include plans; boats for hire on the lake and children's boating pond; summer weekend bandstand music; open-air theatre and musicals Jun–Sep ☎ 020 7486 2431 (box office)

Regent's Park has everything an urban explorer could wish for: big open spaces, a lake to row on, spectacular gardens, ducks and swans in quantity, ideal picnic spots and alfresco theatre and music.

The Prince's plan Regent's Park is the result of a remarkable coincidence of royal enlightenment, architectural theatre, peaceful times and a large tract of land becoming available. In 1811 the Prince Regent, later George IV, and his architect, John Nash, conceived and completed a Regency backbone for London stretching from St. James's Park up Regent Street and Portland Place to Regent's Park. After vast earth-moving activities, the park was given its undulating lawns, lake, garden and trees, all ringed by grand terrace backdrops and dotted with just eight of the 56 planned villas.

From nobles to the people What was designed as a garden city for nobles is now the most elegant of London parks. It has been open to the public since 1835, when Regent's Canal was one of the busiest stretches of canal in Britain. Londoners flocked to visit the zoo, Inner Circle (later Queen Mary's) Gardens and Avenue Gardens, which W. A. Nesfield designed in 1864. Its 197ha (487 acres) easily absorb the many Muslims strolling from the gold-domed Central Mosque, patrons of the Open Air Theatre, cricketers—and many others besides.

The canal at Little Venice

London Zoo

London Zoo is not overly large but it's a good idea to plan your day around the timetable of activities, such as feeding times, talks, shows and the enjoyable Animals in Action presentations, to get the best from your visit.

Exotic animals for Londoners In 1826 Sir Stamford Raffles, who established Singapore Colony, founded the Zoological Society of London with Sir Humphry Davy. Four years later it opened 2ha (5 acres) of its gardens to the public, and met with immediate success. The Society's own collection of exotic animals —zebras, monkeys, kangaroos and bears—was soon enlarged by the royal menagerie from Windsor Castle and the royal zoo from the Tower of London.

Extraordinary animals Over the years new arrivals have included Tommy the chimpanzee in 1835 and, in 1836, the giraffes, which set a trend for giraffe-patterned fabric. Jumbo and Alice, the African elephants, were also exceedingly popular with visitors. Meanwhile, the world's first reptile house, aquarium and insect houses were constructed.

A modern zoo Aware of the worldwide controversy over zoos, London Zoo is maintaining its place at the forefront of animal conservation and education. It houses the Institute of Zoology, which carries out research, and funds important ground-breaking fieldwork. The Children's Zoo has a 'petting paddock' and an area to teach children how to care for pets. While deer roam, lions roar and birds screech, there are talks, demonstrations and the Web of Life conservation centre to encourage awareness of the earth's fragility.

HIGHLIGHTS

- Arriving by boat from Camden Lock
- Children's petting zoo
- 50 endangered species
- Penguin Pool
- Reversed lighting to see nocturnal mammals
- Feeding time for lions
- Cavorting chimpanzees
- Web of Life centre

INFORMATION

www.londonzoo.co.uk

- ✚ E2 (for entrance); Locator map B1
- ✉ Regent's Park, NW1
- ☎ 020 7722 3333
- ⏰ Mar–end Oct daily 10–5.30, Nov–end Feb 10–4 (last admission one hour before closing)
- 🍴 Restaurant, cafés and kiosks
- Ⓒ Camden Town
- Ⓒ Camden Town
- ♿ Good
- 💷 Expensive
- ↔ Regent's Park (► 32)
- ❓ Lectures, talks, workshops, regular animal feeding times; animal action programmes daily; animal adoption schemes. The London Waterbus Company runs scheduled servies from Camden Lock and Little Venice

Buckingham Palace

HIGHLIGHTS

- Liveried beadles in the Queen's Gallery
- Changing of the Guard
- State Coach, Royal Mews
- Nash's façade, Quadrangle
- Gobelin tapestries in the Guard Room
- Throne Room
- Van Dyck's portrait of Charles I and family
- Table of Grand Commanders, Blue Drawing Room
- Gilded and painted grand piano (1856)

INFORMATION

www.royal.gov.uk

✚ F6; Locator map C3

✉ Buckingham Gate, SW1

☎ 020 7766 7300; Queen's Gallery 020 7321 2233

◉ Queen's Gallery daily 10–5, last admission 4.30); Royal Mews Mar–end Oct daily 11–4 (also Aug–end Sep 10–5), last admission 45 mins before closing. Closed Ascot week and ceremonial occasions. State Rooms, Buckingham Palace daily 9.30–4.15, Aug–Sep (timed ticket every 15 mins)

◉ Victoria, Hyde Park Corner or Green Park

🚇 Victoria ♿ Excellent

💷 Expensive

❷ No photography

Of the London houses now open to visitors, the Queen's own home is perhaps the most fascinating of all: Where else can you see a living sovereign's private art, drawing rooms and horse harnesses?

Yet another palace The British sovereigns have moved around London quite a bit over the years; from Westminster to Whitehall to Kensington and St. James's, and finally to Buckingham Palace. It was George III who in 1762 bought the prime-site mansion, Buckingham House, as a gift for his new bride, the 17-year-old Queen Charlotte, leaving St. James's Palace to be the official royal residence.

Grand improvements When the Prince Regent finally became King George IV in 1820, he and his architect, John Nash, made extravagant changes using honey-coloured Bath stone, all to be covered up by Edward Blore's façade added for Queen Victoria. Today, the 600 rooms and 16-ha (40-acre) garden include the State Apartments, offices for the Royal Household, a cinema, swimming pool and the Queen's private rooms overlooking Green Park.

Queen Elizabeth II opens her home The Queen inherited the world's finest private art collection. The Queen's Gallery, beautifully remodelled by John Simpson, and opened for the Golden Jubilee in 2002, exhibits some of her riches. In the Royal Mews, John Nash's stables house gleaming fairytale coaches, harnesses and other apparel for royal ceremonies. Make sure you do not miss the Buckingham Palace Summer Opening, when visitors can wander through the grand State Rooms, resplendent with gold, pictures, porcelain, tapestries and thrones.

St. James's Park

Even if you drop in to St. James's Park merely to eat a sandwich and laze on a deck chair while listening to the band's music, you can usually spot a trio of palaces across the duck-filled lake and over the tips of the weeping willows.

Royal through and through St. James's Park is the oldest and most thoroughly royal of London's nine royal parks, surrounded by the Palace of Westminster, St. James's Palace, Buckingham Palace and the remains of Whitehall Palace. Kings and their courtiers have been frolicking here since Henry VIII laid out a deer park in 1532 and built a hunting lodge that became St. James's Palace. James I began the menagerie, which included pelicans, crocodiles and an elephant who drank a gallon of wine daily.

French order Charles II, influenced by Versailles, near Paris, redesigned the park to include a canal (where he swam), Birdcage Walk (where he kept his aviaries) and the gravelled Mall, where he played pell mell, a courtly French game similar to croquet. Then George IV, helped by John Nash and influenced by Humphry Repton, softened the garden's formal French lines into the English style, making this 37-ha (93-acre) park of blossoming shrubs and undulating, curving paths popular with all romantics.

Nature dominates As the park is an important migration point and breeding area for birds, two full-time ornithologists look after up to 1,000 birds from more than 45 species. Among the fig, plane and willow trees, seek out the pelicans living on Duck Island, a tradition begun when the Russian Ambassador gave some to Charles II.

HIGHLIGHTS

- Springtime daffodils
- Whitehall from the lake bridge
- Feeding the pelicans, 3pm
- Views to Buckingham Palace
- Duck Island in springtime

INFORMATION

- ✚ F6; Locator map C3
- ✉ The Mall, SW1
- ☎ 020 7930 1793
- ⏰ Daily dawn to midnight
- 🍴 Inn the Park (➤ 64)
- Ⓜ St. James's Park, Green Park, or Westminster
- 🚉 Victoria
- ♿ Very good
- 🎟 Free
- ↔ Buckingham Palace (➤ 34), Banqueting House (➤ 39)
- ❓ Changing the Guard (contact tourist information). Occasional bird talks; summer bandstand music

The Whitehall skyline seen from the park

Tate Britain

INFORMATION

www.tate.org.uk

- G8; Locator map D3
- Millbank, SW1, entrances on Millbank and Atterbury Street
- 020 7887 8000
- Daily 10–5.50
- Restaurant, café
- Pimlico, Vauxhall or Westminster
- Victoria
- Very good
- Free except for special exhibitions
- Westminster Abbey (► 37)
- Full education programme; audio tours

Moving through the galleries past Gainsborough portraits, Turner landscapes and Hepworth sculptures, this is an intimate social history of Britain told by its painters.

Two for one   The Tate Gallery was opened in 1897, named after the sugar millionaire Henry Tate, who paid for the core building and donated his Victorian pictures to put inside it. Until 2000, the national collections of British and international modern art were housed there, with increasingly inadequate space. Then, the international modern collection went to Bankside Power Station and was renamed Tate Modern (► 47). The national collection now fills Henry Tate's refurbished building, completed in October 2001, which is renamed Tate Britain.

British art   Recognizing that many people are unfamiliar with British art, the galleries are helpfully divided into four chronological suites. You can follow the visual story of British art from 1500 until today. Although paintings, sculptures, installations and works in other media will be changed regularly, you may well see Nicholas Hilliard's icon-like portrait of Elizabeth I, Van Dyck's lavish court portraits, and richly coloured Pre-Raphaelite canvases. Do not miss the great Turner collection housed in the adjoining Clore Gallery.

The Turner Prize   Britain's most prestigious and controversial prize to celebrate young British talent is run by the Tate and awarded each autumn following an exhibition of nominees' works. Founded in 1984, winners have included Damien Hurst and Chris Ofili, while Gilbert and George, Tracey Emin, Sam Taylor-Wood and Tony Cragg have all been nominees.

Westminster Abbey

The very best time to be in the abbey is for the 8am service, sometimes held in tiny St. Faith's Chapel, followed by a wander in the silent nave and cloisters before the crowds arrive.

The kernel of London's second city It was Edward the Confessor who in the 11th century began the rebuilding of the modest Benedictine abbey church of St. Peter, which was consecrated in 1065. The first sovereign to be crowned there was William the Conqueror, on Christmas Day 1066. Successive kings were patrons, as were the pilgrims who flocked to the Confessor's shrine. Henry III (1216–72) employed Master Henry de Reyns to re-begin the Gothic abbey that

The West Front

stands today, and Henry VII (1485–1509) built his Tudor chapel with its delicate fan vaulting. Since William I, all sovereigns have been crowned here—even after Henry VIII broke with Rome in 1533 and made himself head of the Church of England; and all were buried here up to George II (after which Windsor became the royal burial place ▶ 21).

Daunting riches The abbey is massive, full of monuments and very popular. From the nave's west end enjoy the view and Master Henry's achievement, then look over the Victorian Gothic choir screen into Henry V's chantry. Having explored the chapels, the royal necropolis and Poets' Corner, leave time for the quiet cloisters.

HIGHLIGHTS

- Poet's Corner
- Sir Isaac Newton memorial
- Sir James Thornhill's window
- Henry VII's Chapel
- Edward the Confessor's Chapel
- St. Faith's Chapel
- Tomb of the Unknown Warrior
- Little Cloister and College Garden
- Weekday sung evensong at 5pm

INFORMATION

www.westminster-abbey.org
- G7; Locator map D3
- Broad Sanctuary, SW1; entry by North Door
- 020 7222 5152
- Abbey Mon–Fri 9.30–3.45, Sat 9.30–1.45 (also Wed until 7); no photography. Chapter House, Pyx Chamber (currently closed), Abbey Museum, College Garden daily various hours. Closed before special services, Sun, 24–25 Dec Good Fri and Commonwealth Day
- Café in cloisters
- Westminster, St. James's Park
- Victoria Good
- Services free. Royal Chapels moderate
- Guided tours, audio guides

Houses of Parliament

INFORMATION

www.parliament.uk

✚ G7; Locator map D3

✉ Westminster, SW1

☎ 020 7219 3000;
Commons 020 7219 4272;
Lords 020 7219 3107;
Jewel Tower 020 7222 2219

◉ Visits to House of Commons when house is sitting Mon 2.30–late, Tue–Wed 11.30–7.30, Thu 11.30–6.30, Fri 9.30–3. Tours during summer recesses (Jul to end Oct), call for details. Non-UK residents can apply for tickets from their embassy or consulate. Jewel Tower Apr–end Sep daily 10–6; Oct 10–5; Nov–end Mar 10–4

🚇 Westminster 🚉 Waterloo

♿ Parliament free; tours expensive. Jewel Tower moderate

❓ State Opening of Parliament mid-Nov

Big Ben is for many the symbol of London: They love its tower, its huge clear clockface and its thundering hour bell. Summer tours of the whole building reveal its beauty, intriguing traditions and government workings.

Powerhouse for Crown and State   William the Conqueror made Westminster his seat of rule to watch over the London merchants (he also built the Tower of London ➤ 50). It was soon the heart of government for England, then Britain, then a globe-encircling empire. It was also the principal home of the monarchs until Henry VIII moved to Whitehall.

Mother of parliaments   Here the foundations of Parliament were laid according to Edward I's Model Parliament of 1295; a combination of elected citizens, lords and clergy. This developed into the House of Commons (elected Members of Parliament) and the House of Lords (unelected senior members of State and Church). Henry VIII's Reformation Parliament of 1529–36 ended Church domination of Parliament and made the Commons more powerful than the Lords.

A building fit for an empire   Having survived the Catholic conspiracy to blow up Parliament (on 5 November 1605, Guy Fawkes' night), almost all the buildings were destroyed by a fire in 1834. Kingdom and empire needed a new headquarters. With Charles Barry's plans and A. W. Pugin's detailed design, a masterpiece of Victorian Gothic was created. Behind the river façade decorated with statues of rulers, the Lords is on the left and the Commons on the right. If Parliament is in session, there is a flag on Victoria Tower or, at night, a light on Big Ben.

Banqueting House

It is chilling to imagine Charles I calmly walking across the park from St. James's Palace to be beheaded outside the glorious hall built by his father. The magnificent ceiling was painted for Charles by Peter Paul Rubens.

London's most magnificent room This, all that remains of Whitehall Palace, was London's first building to be coated in smooth, white Portland stone. Designed by Inigo Jones and built between 1619 and 1622, it marked the beginning of James I's dream to replace the original sprawling Tudor palace with a 2,000-room Palladian masterpiece. In fact, it was only the banqueting hall that was built. Inside, the King hosted small parties in the crypt and presided over lavish court ceremonies upstairs.

The Rubens ceiling The stunning ceiling was commissioned by James's son, Charles I. Painted between 1634 and 1636 by Peter Paul Rubens, the leading baroque artist based in Antwerp, the panels celebrate James I, who was also James VI of Scotland. Nine allegorical paintings show the unification of Scotland and England and the joyous benefits of wise rule. Rubens was paid £3,000 and given a knighthood for the work.

The demise of Whitehall Palace This palace has brought a fair share of bad luck to its occupants. Cardinal Thomas Wolsey lived so ostentatiously that he fell from Henry VIII's favour. Henry moved in, making it his and his successors' main London royal residence. It was here that Charles I was beheaded on 30 January 1649, and William III suffered from the dank river air. A fire in 1698 wiped out the Tudor building, leaving only the stone Banqueting House.

HIGHLIGHTS

- Sculpted head of Charles I
- Weathercock put on the roof by James II
- Rubens ceiling
- Allegory of James I between Peace and Plenty
- Allegory of the birth and coronation of Charles I
- Lunchtime concerts
- Whitehall river terrace in Embankment Gardens
- The video and self-guiding audio tour

INFORMATION

www.hrp.org.uk
- G6; Locator map D3
- Whitehall, SW1
- 020 7930 4179
- Mon–Sat 10–5; last admission 4.30. Closed 24 Dec–1 Jan, public hols and for functions
- Westminster, Charing Cross or Embankment
- None
- Moderate
- Occasional lunchtime concerts

Inigo Jones's façade

National Portrait Gallery

HIGHLIGHTS

- *Self-portrait with Barbara Hepworth*, Ben Nicholson
- Icon-like *Richard II*
- The Tudor Galleries
- *Samuel Pepys*, John Hayl
- *Queen Victoria*, Sir George Hayter
- *The Brontë Sisters*, Branwell Brontë
- *Isambard Kingdom Brunel*, John Callcott
- *Florence Nightingale*, William White
- *Sir Peter Hall*, Tom Phillips
- Using the self-guiding audio tour
- An unfinished sketch of Jane Austen (c1810) by her sister, Cassandra

INFORMATION

www.npg.org.uk

🔢 G5; Locator map C2

✉ St. Martin's Place, WC2

☎ 020 7306 0055

🕐 Daily 10–6 (also Thu–Fri until 9pm); closed Good Fri

🍴 Café, rooftop restaurant

🚇 Leicester Square or Charing Cross

🚉 Charing Cross

♿ Good

🎟 Free except for special exhibitions

↔ National Gallery (➤ 41)

❓ Lectures, events

It is always fascinating to see what someone famous looks like and how they chose to be painted—for instance, you would never expect Francis Drake to be in red courtier's, rather than sailor's, clothes.

A British record Founded in 1856 to collect portraits of the great and good in British life, and so inspire others to greatness, this now huge collection is the world's most comprehensive of its kind. There are oil paintings, watercolours, caricatures, silhouettes and photographs.

Start at the top The galleries, incorporating a new wing, are arranged in chronological order, starting on the top floor—reached by stairs or elevator. Tudor monarchs kick off a visual Who's Who of British history that moves through inventors, merchants, engineers, explorers and empire builders to modern politicians, always accompanied by their observers, the writers. Here you'll find Isambard K. Brunel, Robert Clive and Warren Hastings of India, Winston Churchill and Margaret Thatcher. There is Chaucer in his floppy hat, Kipling at his desk and A. A. Milne with Christopher Robin and Winnie-the-Pooh on his knee. Lesser-known sitters also merit a close look, such as the 18th-century portrait of the extensive Sharp Family, who formed an orchestra and played at Fulham every Sunday.

A modern record, too At first, the Victorians insisted upon entry only after death, but this rule has been broken. Among the many contemporary portraits, you may find those of the football star David Beckham, Beatle Sir Paul McCartney, actors John Hurt and Stephen Fry, painter Patrick Heron and Joan Collins.

National Gallery

Here is a collection of tip-top pictures—and for free, so you can drop in for a few minutes' peace in front of Leonardo da Vinci's cartoon in the Sainsbury Wing or Rubens's ravishing *Samson and Delilah*.

A quality collection Founded in 1824 with just 38 pictures, the National Gallery now has about 2,000 paintings, all on show. Spread throughout William Wilkins's neoclassical building and the Sainsbury Wing extension (opened 1991), they provide an uncramped, extremely high-quality, concise panorama of European painting from Giotto to Cézanne. Most modern and British pictures are at the Tate Galleries (➤ 36, 47).

Free from the start Unusually for a national painting collection, the nucleus is not royal but the collection of John Julius Angerstein, a self-made financier. From the start it was open to all, including children, free of charge, and provided a wide spectrum of British painting within a European context—aims that are still maintained. However, there is a charge for the usually excellent temporary exhibitions in the Sainsbury Wing.

A first visit To take advantage of the rich artistic panorama, why not choose a room from each of the four chronologically arranged sections? Early paintings by Duccio di Buoninsegna, Jan van Eyck, Piero della Francesca and others fill the Sainsbury Wing. The West Wing has 16th-century pictures, including Michelangelo's *Entombment*, while the North Wing is devoted to 17th-century artists such as Van Dyck, Rubens, Rembrandt, Velàzquez and painters of the Dutch school. Finally, the East Wing runs from Chardin through Gainsborough to Matisse and Picasso.

HIGHLIGHTS

- *Virgin Enthroned*, Cenni di Peppi Cimabue
- Cartoon, Leonardo da Vinci
- *Pope Julius II*, Raphael
- *The Arnolfini Wedding*, Van Eyck
- Equestrian portrait of Charles I by Van Dyck
- *The Haywain*, John Constable
- *Madonna of the Pinks*, Raphael
- *The Archers*, Henry Raeburn
- *Sunflowers*, Van Gogh
- *Mr and Mrs William Hallett*, Gainsborough
- *La Pointe de Hève*, Monet
- View from Wilkins's entrance

INFORMATION

www.nationalgallery.org.uk
- 🔢 G6; Locator map C2
- ✉ Trafalgar Square, WC2
- ☎ 020 7747 2885
- 🕐 Mon, Tue, Thu–Sun 10–6, Wed 10–9; late openings for some special exhibitions. Closed Good Fri
- 🍴 Brasserie, basement café
- Ⓜ Charing Cross or Leicester Square
- 🚆 Charing Cross
- ♿ Excellent
- 💷 Free except for special exhibitions
- ❓ Guided tours (free daily 11.30 and 3.30, also Wed 6.30), lectures, films, audio guide

41

British Airways London Eye

London's most visible attraction, soaring 135m (443ft) above the south bank of the Thames, is the world's largest observation wheel and affords spectacular views of the city.

HIGHLIGHTS

- Panoramic views across the city in every direction
- On a clear day you can see for 40km (25 miles)
- Views of the Thames
- Aerial view of Palace of Westminster

INFORMATION

www.ba-londoneye.com
- G6; Locator map D3
- Jubilee Gardens, South Bamk, SE1
- 0870 990 8883; booking 0870 500 0600
- Daily 9.30am–8pm, (also May–end Sep Fri–Sat 9.30–9) Opening times may vary; make sure you arrive 30 mins before your flight
- Café in Jubilee Gardens
- Waterloo, Westminster, Embankment or Charing Cross
- Waterloo
- Very good. Boarding ramp available for wheelchair users
- Expensive
- Westminster Abbey (► 37), Houses of Parliament (► 38)

Riding high Passengers ride in one of the 32 capsules that rotate smoothly through 360 degrees in a slow-moving, 30-minute flight. Each capsule is fully enclosed and comfortably holds 25 people. Because the capsules are secured on the outside of the wheel (rather than hung from it like a Ferris Wheel), views through the large glass windows are totally unobstructed. Passengers can walk freely inside the capsules, which are kept level by a motorized motion stability system—although seating is provided. Each capsule is in touch with the ground via camera and radio links. The wheel is in constant motion, revolving continuously at 0.26m (0.85ft) per second, a quarter of the average walking speed, enabling passengers to walk straight on and off the moving capsules. After dark, the trees lining the approach to the London Eye are bathed in green lights, while the boarding platform appears to float on a cloud of blue light.

Revolutionary design Conceived by David Marks and Julia Barfield to celebrate the millennium, the Eye represents the turning of the century and is a universal and ancient symbol of regeneration. It took seven years and the expertize of people from five European countries for their design to be realized.

Back on the ground The Eye marks the start of the riverside Jubilee Walk that reaches right up to Tower Bridge. It has also helped to revitalize a forgotten corner of London; nearby are the London Aquarium and the Saatchi Gallery.

Somerset House

Transformed from a lavish but forgotten building into a riverside palace, spend a day here moving from French Impressionist masterpieces to English silver to some of Russia's finest art.

A palatial home A majestic, triple-arched gateway leads from the Strand into Sir William Chamber's English Palladian government offices (1776–86). Within the gateway, the Courtauld Collection is housed in rooms lavishly decorated for the Royal Academy, before its move to Piccadilly. Ahead, the great courtyard has fountains, a theatre, an ice-rink and café tables, according to the season. The rooms overlooking the Thames, accessed from the courtyard or from the Embankment, contain a restaurant, café and two special interest treats: The Gilbert Collection and the Hermitage Rooms.

The Courtauld Gallery A stunning collection of French Impressionist paintings—Manet, Renoir, Cezanne, Van Gogh, Gaugin—collected by the industrialist Samuel Courtauld inspired six other collectors to donate art. So the art feast also has Italian Renaissance panels, Rubens canvases and Ben Nicholsons.

The Gilbert Collection Arthur Gilbert, born in London, made his fortune in California and spent it on art in three fields: Roman and Florentine mosaics, gold and silverware and 18th-century gold snuff boxes. Then he gave it all to his home town.

The Hermitage Rooms An outpost of the State Hermitage Museum in St. Petersburg, the 500 or so exhibits selected from its astoundingly rich collection change regularly, so you really need to drop in to see what's new on each visit.

HIGHLIGHTS

Courtauld Collection:
- The Fridart Collection
- *Bar at the Folies-Bergere*, Manet
- A roomful of Rubens paintings
- *The Trinity*, Botticelli

Gilbert Collection:
- Micro-mosaic table top with views of Rome
- Silver ewer, Paul de Lamerie
- 18th-century enamel snuff boxes

INFORMATION

www.somersethouse.org.uk
- G5; Locator map D2
- Somerset House, Strand, WC2
- 020 7845 4600
- Daily 10–6; extended hours for Courtyard, River Terrace and restaurant. Courtauld Institute Gallery last admission 5.15; Gilbert Collection last admission 5.30; Hermitage Rooms last admission 5
- Cafés, restaurant
- Temple (closed Sun)
- Blackfriars, Charing Cross
- Excellent
- Somerset House free; Courtauld, Gilbert and Hermitage moderate
- Sir John Soane's Musuem (► 44), Dr. Johnson's House (► 54)

43

Sir John Soane's Museum

HIGHLIGHTS

- *The Rake's Progress, The Election*, Hogarth
- Sarcophagus of Seti I
- Lawrence's portrait of Soane
- Monk's Parlour
- Works by Turner, Canaletto
- Model Room

INFORMATION

www.soane.org

- ✚ G5; Locator map D2
- ✉ 13 Lincoln's Inn Fields, WC2
- ☎ 020 7405 2107
- 🕐 Tue–Sat 10–5 (also 1st Tue of the month 10am–9pm); closed 24–26 Dec, 1 Jan, Good Fri
- Ⓗ Holborn, Chancery Lane (closed Sun)
- 🚃 Farringdon
- 🎫 Free
- ⬌ Somerset House (➤ 43), British Museum (➤ 45), Dickens House (➤ 54)
- 🛈 Guided tours Sat 2.30

As you move about the gloriously over-furnished rooms of Soane's two houses and into the calm upstairs drawing room, his presence is so strong you feel you would not be surprised if he were there to greet you.

Soane the architect   This double treasure-house in leafy Lincoln's Inn Fields, central London's largest square, is where the neoclassical architect Sir John Soane lived. First he designed No. 12 and lived there from 1792. Then he bought No. 13 next door, rebuilt it with cunningly proportioned rooms, and lived there from 1813 until his death in 1837. Meanwhile, he also designed Holy Trinity church on Marylebone Road (1824–48), and parts of the Treasury, Whitehall. His model for his masterpiece, the (destroyed) Bank of England, is here (re-created rooms now form the bank's museum ➤ 52). No. 14 opens as a centre for Adam Studies in late 2005.

Soane the collector   Soane was an avid collector. He found that every art object could inspire his work, so his rooms were a visual reference library. Hogarth's paintings unfold from the walls in layers. There are so many sculptures, paintings and antiquities that unless you keep your eyes peeled you will miss a Watteau drawing, a Greek vase or something better.

The ghost of Soane   Sir John's ingenious designs pervade every room, as do the stories of his passion for collecting. For example, when an Egyptian sarcophagus arrived, he gave a three-day party in its honour.

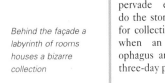

Behind the façade a labyrinth of rooms houses a bizarre collection

British Museum

It's fun to choose your own seven wonders of the world in the British Museum. It's likely the bronzes from the Indian Chola dynasty and the lion-filled reliefs that once lined an Assyrian palace will be on the list.

The physician founder   Sir Hans Sloane, after whom Sloane Square is named, was a fashionable London physician, 'interested in the whole of human knowledge' and an avid collector of everything from plants to prints. When he died in 1753 aged 92 he left his collection of more than 80,000 objects to the nation on condition that it was given a permanent home. Thus began the British Museum, opened in 1759 in a 17th-century mansion, Britain's first public museum and now its largest, covering 5.5ha (13.5 acres).

It grew and it grew   To Sloane's collection were added many others. Kings George II, III and IV made magnificent gifts, as did other monarchs. These, with the Townley and Elgin Marbles, burst the building's seams and the architect Robert Smirke designed a grand new museum, completed by his son, Sydney, in 1857. Even so, because the booty from expeditions and excavations poured in continuously, the Natural History collections went to South Kensington (► 28). With the departure of the British Library (► 56) to St. Pancras in 1998, the Great Court has been redeveloped, the Sainsbury Galleries built and the King's Library restored.

Coming to grips with the British Museum   A good way to explore 'that old curiosity shop in Great Russell Street' is to pick up a plan in the Great Court, see what special events are on, choose at the most three rooms to see and set off to find them. For peace and quiet, go early.

HIGHLIGHTS

- Oriental antiquities
- Sainsbury Galleries
- Rosetta Stone
- Current prints and drawings
- Islamic Art
- Mildenhall and Sutton Hoo treasures
- Elgin Marbles
- Assyrian and Egyptian rooms
- The King's Library
- Norman Foster's Great Court redevelopment

INFORMATION

www.thebritishmuseum.ac.uk
- G4; Locator map D2
- Great Russell Street, WC1 (another entrance in Montague Place)
- 020 7323 8783
- Sat–Wed 10–5.30, Thu, Fri 10–8.30. Great Court Mon–Wed, Sun 9–6, Thu–Sat 9am–11pm
- Restaurant, cafés
- Holborn or Tottenham Court Road
- Very good
- Free except for some temporary exhibitions, tours and late openings
- Percival David Foundation of Chinese Art (► 53)
- Full educational programme

45

St. Paul's Cathedral

HIGHLIGHTS

- Sung evensong
- Frescos and mosaics
- Wren's Great Model in the riforium (upstairs)
- Triple-layered dome weighing 76,000 tons
- Jean Tijou's sanctuary gates
- Wellington's memorial
- *Light of the World*, Holman Hunt
- The great climb
- Wren's epitaph under the dome

INFORMATION

www.stpauls.co.uk

To sneak into St. Paul's for afternoon evensong, and sit gazing up at the mosaics as the choir's voices soar, is to savour a moment of absolute peace and beauty. Go early or late to avoid the crowds.

Wren's London After the restoration of the monarchy in 1660, artistic patronage bloomed under Charles II. Then, when the Great Fire of London destroyed four-fifths of the City in 1666, Christopher Wren took centre stage, being appointed King's Surveyor-General in 1669, aged just 37. The spires, towers and steeples of his 51 new churches (23 still stand) surrounded his masterpiece, St. Paul's.

The fifth St. Paul's This cathedral church for the diocese of London was founded in AD604 by King Ethelbert of Kent. The first four churches burned down. Wren's, built in stone and paid for with a special coal tax, was the first English cathedral built by a single architect, the only one with a dome, and the only one in the English baroque style. In 2005 it emerges from a total clean, inside and out, as pristine as the day the building was completed. Statues and memorials of Britain's famous crowd the interior and crypt.

The great climb The 530 steps to the top are worth the effort. Shallow steps (259) rise to the Whispering Gallery for good views of Sir James Thornhill's dome frescos and the 19th-century mosaics. The external Stone Gallery has telescopes and benches; above is the Golden Gallery.

Tate Modern

The national collection of modern art fills the magnificent spaces of George Gilbert Scott's monumental Bankside Power Station by the Thames, making it London's most radical new focus for the new millennium.

World Class Art On a par with the Metropolitan Museum of Modern Art in New York in its range, richness and quality, the collection that once shared space with the British Collection (▶ 36) now blossoms in its own huge spaces. Swiss architects Herzog & de Meuron have created an exciting contemporary structure within the handsome brick building, making it ideal for exhibiting large-scale works of art in an innovative way. Gallery events, cafés, a big shop and a rooftop restaurant complete the total package for a great day out and a focal point for the now rejuvenated South Bank.

20th century and more Works exhibited here continue the story of art begun by the National Gallery. The most influential artists of the 20th century are all represented, including Picasso, Matisse, Dali, Duchamp, Rodin, Gabo and Warhol—as well as British artists such as Bacon, Hodgkin, Hockney and Caro. Works on display change regularly, and there are special exhibitions. But together they represent all the major periods and movements of the 20th century, from Surrealism to Conceptual Art.

Daringly contemporary Tate Modern is itself a modern building in an old skin. It connects to the north bank via the Millennium Bridge. It augments its collection with the cutting edge of contemporary art, and even its display methods are new. Four suites of rooms, each devoted to one subject, mix together pieces from various periods.

HIGHLIGHTS

Although displays change, look out for works by:
- Pablo Picasso
- Claude Monet
- Henri Matisse
- Constantin Brancusi
- Jackson Pollock
- Mark Rothko
- Bridget Riley
- Marcel Duchamp
- Andy Warhol
- Richard Hamilton
- David Hockney

INFORMATION

www.tate.org.uk
- J6; Locator map E2
- Bankside, SE1
- 020 7887 8000
- Sun–Thu 10–6, Fri–Sat 10–10
- Cafés, restaurant
- Blackfriars or Southwark
- Blackfriars or London Bridge
- Very good
- Free, charge for some special exhibitions
- Shakespeare's Globe (▶ 22), St. Paul's Cathedral (▶ 46), The Tower of London (▶ 50), Southwark Cathedral (▶ 22, 57), London Eye (▶ 42)
- Full educational programme. Choice of free daily audio tours

St. Bartholomew-the-Great

INFORMATION

- ✚ J4; Locator map E2
- ✉ West Smithfield, EC1
- ☎ 0206 7606 5171
- 🕐 Mon–Fri 8.30–5 (winter until 4), Sat 10.30–1, Sun 2–8pm.
  Sun services 9am, 11am, 6.30 (choral)
- 🚇 Barbican, Farringdon or St. Paul's
- 🚆 Farringdon
- ♿ Good
- 💷 Free (donation encouraged)
- ↔ St. Paul's Cathedral (► 46), Museum of London (► 49)

A Sunday evening spent at St. Bartholomew's is truly memorable: While trucks arrive at Smithfield's meat market, you can answer the ringing bells and pass under the great stone arch into a hidden, medieval world.

A court jester for founder Henry I's court jester, Rahere, became an Augustinian canon. While on pilgrimage to Rome he was cured of malaria, had a vision of St. Bartholomew and took a vow. On his return, the King gave him land to found St. Bartholomew's Hospital and Priory—London's first hospital but one of four monasteries in the area.

London's oldest church Rahere's priory church, built in 1123, is London's oldest surviving church, the City's only 12th-century monastic church, and its best surviving piece of large-scale Romanesque architecture. The remains (the nave and cloisters are gone) give an idea of the magnificence of London's dozen or so medieval monastic churches.

Entering a different world The church lies through a 13th-century stone arch topped by a Tudor gatehouse, which once led into the great priory church's west end. Today, a path runs the length of what was the ten-bay nave, down to the present west door. Here is the choir, the ambulatory and the Lady Chapel (built by Rahere), whose roofs are supported by honey-coloured walls and sturdy, circular columns. The minimal decoration makes the impact all the more powerful. Two tombs sit uneasily together here: those of the founder, Rahere (*d*1143; tomb 1404), and of the destroyer, Richard Rich, who bought the building from Henry VIII after the dissolution of the monasteries.

Museum of London

A visit here is easily the best way to cruise through London's 2,000 years of history, pausing to see a Roman shoe, the Lord Mayor's State Coach or an old shop counter; and it is even built on the West Gate of London's Roman fort.

A museum for London This is the world's largest and most comprehensive city museum, opened in 1976 in a building by Powell and Moya. The collection combines the old Guildhall Museum's City antiquities with the London Museum's costumes and other culturally related objects. Plenty of building work and redevelopment in the City of London since the 1980s, allied with increased awareness about conservation, has ensured a steady flow of archaeological finds into the collection.

A museum about London The story of London is long and can be confusing. The building is, appropriately, in the barbican of the Roman fort, and the rooms are laid out chronologically to keep the story clear. The London Before London gallery follows the story of prehistoric Londoners before Roman settlement. One of the most impressive galleries is Roman London, which explains the founding of Londinium in about AD50 until AD410 when the Roman army quit Britain. The World City galleries cover the period from the French Revolution to the outbreak of World War I. Most of the £33 million redevelopment is now open—and impressive. See especially the London Before London Gallery.

A museum about Londoners People make a city, so in every room it is Londoners who are really telling the story, whether it is through their Roman storage jars, their Tudor leather clothes or their Suffragette posters.

HIGHLIGHTS

- London Before London Gallery
- Hoard of 43 gold Roman coins
- Sptialfields Woman (Roman)
- Viking grave
- Fragments from the Eleanor Cross
- Tudor jewellery
- Model of Tudor London
- Pepys's chess set
- 17th-century panelled room
- World City Gallery

INFORMATION

www.museumoflondon.org.uk
- 🔲 J4; Locator map E2
- ✉ 150 London Wall, EC2
- ☎ 0870 444 3852; recorded information 0870 444 3851
- 🕐 Mon–Sat 10–5.50, Sun noon–5.50. Closed 24–26 Dec, 1 Jan
- 🍴 Café
- Ⓖ Barbican, Moorgate or St. Paul's
- 🚇 Moorgate, Farringdon, Liverpool Street or City Thameslink
- 🚻 Excellent 🆓 Free
- ↔ St. Paul's Cathedral (➤ 46), St. Bartholomew the Great (➤ 48), Barbican (➤ 80–81)
- ❓ Full education programme; audio tour

Mural depicting a scene from the Great Fire

49

HM The Tower of London

HIGHLIGHTS

- Medieval Palace
- Raleigh's room
- Imperial State Crown
- Tower ravens
- Grand Punch Bowl, 1829
- St. John's Chapel

INFORMATION

www.hrp.org.uk
- ✚ K5; Locator map F2
- ✉ Tower Hill, EC3
- ☎ 0870 756 6060
- 🕐 Mar–end Oct Mon–Sat 9–6, Sun 10–6, (last admission 5); Nov–end Feb Tue–Sat 9–5, Sun–Mon 10–5 (last admission 4)
- 🍴 Cafés, restaurant
- Ⓜ Tower Hill
- 🚉 Fenchurch Street, London Bridge or Docklands Light Railway (Tower Gateway)
- ♿ Excellent for Jewel House
- 💷 Expensive
- ❓ Free guided tours every 30 minutes; audio tours

A 'Beefeater'

The restored rooms of Edward I's 13th-century palace bring the Tower alive as the royal palace and place of pageantry it was; for some, they are more interesting than the Crown Jewels.

Medieval fortress The Tower of London is Britain's best medieval fortress. William the Conqueror (1066–87) began it as a show of brute force, and Edward I (1272–1307) completed it. William's Caen stone White Tower, built within old Roman walls, was an excellent defence: It was 27m (90ft) high, with walls 4.5m (15ft) thick, and space for soldiers, servants and nobles. Henry III began the Inner Wall, the moat, his own watergate—and the royal zoo. Edward I completed the Inner Wall, built the Outer Wall, several towers and Traitor's Gate, and moved the mint and Crown Jewels here from Westminster.

Scenes of splendour and horror Stephen (1135–54) was the first king to live here, James I (1603–25) the last. From here Edward I went in procession to his coronation and Henry VIII paraded through the city bedecked in cloth of gold. Here the Barons seized the Tower to force King John to put his seal to the Magna Carta in 1215; and here two princes were murdered while their uncle was being crowned Richard III. Since 1485 it has been guarded by Yeoman Warders or 'Beefeaters'.

Seven centuries of history The Tower has been palace, fortress, state prison and execution site. There is much to see. Come early and see the Crown Jewels and the Crowns and Diamonds Exhibition, then take a break along the Wharf.

LONDON's
best

London's Best

Museums & Galleries

DULWICH PICTURE GALLERY

Dulwich Picture Gallery's magnificent core collection of 400 paintings was assembled for the King of Poland's projected national gallery. When the king abdicated, the collection was offered unsuccessfully to Britain for the same purpose. The art dealer who put it together, Noel Desenfans, gave it to Sir Francis Bourgeois, who donated it to Dulwich College. Housed in a building designed by Sir John Soane, and opened in 1814, it was England's first public art gallery. Well worth the journey.

➕ Off map at K10
✉ Gallery Road, SE21
☎ 020 8693 5254
🕐 Tue–Fri 10–5, Sat–Sun 11–5 🍴 Café 🚇 North or West Dulwich 💷 Moderate

The Edwardian Room, in the Geffrye Museum

BANK OF ENGLAND MUSEUM

Britain's monetary and banking system since 1694.
➕ J5 ✉ Bartholomew Lane, EC2 ☎ 020 7601 5491 🕐 Mon–Fri 10–5 🚇 Bank 💷 Free

CABINET WAR ROOMS

The underground headquarters for Sir Winston Churchill's War Cabinet during World War II.
➕ G6 ✉ Clive Steps, King Charles Street, SW1 ☎ 020 7930 6961
🕐 Apr–end Sep daily 9.30–6; Oct–end Mar 10–6 🚇 St. James's Park or Westminster 💷 Moderate

DESIGN MUSEUM

Founded by design guru Sir Terence Conran.
➕ L6 ✉ Butler's Wharf, Shad Thames, SE1 ☎ 020 7403 6933
🕐 Daily 10–5.45 (Fri until 9) 🍴 Café, restaurant 🚇 Tower Hill or London Bridge 🚆 London Bridge 💷 Moderate

GEFFRYE MUSEUM

Furniture and design displayed in old almshouses.
➕ K3 ✉ Kingsland Road, E2 ☎ 020 7739 9893 🕐 Tue–Sat 10–5, Sun noon–5 🍴 Café 🚇 Old Street, bus 243; Liverpool Street, bus 149, 242 💷 Free

HOUSE MUSEUMS (➤ 54)

IMPERIAL WAR MUSEUM

Focuses on the social impact of 20th-century warfare through film, painting and sound archives. The Holocaust Museum is not suitable for children.
➕ H7 ✉ Lambeth Road, SE1
☎ 020 7416 5000 🕐 Daily 10–6 🍴 Restaurant, café 🚇 Lambeth North, Elephant & Castle or Waterloo 🚆 Waterloo 💷 Free

JEWISH MUSEUM

One of two museums devoted to London's Jewish community (the other is in Finchley).

➕ F3 ✉ 129–131 Albert Streert, NW1 ☎ 020 7284 1997 🕐 Mon–Thu 10–4, Sun 10–5 🚇 Camden Town 🎫 Moderate

MUSEUM IN DOCKLANDS

A host of objects and displays tell the story of London's river, port and people from Roman times until the present day.

➕ Off map from N5 ✉ No. 1 Warehouses, West India Quay, Canary Wharf, E14 ☎ 0870 444 3857/3856 🕐 Daily 10–6 🍴 Restaurant 🚇 West India Quay 🎫 Moderate

PERCIVAL DAVID FOUNDATION OF CHINESE ART

Sublime Chinese ceramics.

➕ G4 ✉ 53 Gordon Square, WC1 ☎ 020 7387 3909 🕐 Mon–Fri 10.30–5 🚇 Russell Square 🎫 Free

PHOTOGRAPHERS' GALLERY

Contemporary photos in the heart of London.

➕ G5 ✉ 5–8 Great Newport Street, WC2 ☎ 020 7831 1772 🕐 Mon–Sat 11–6, Sun noon–6 🚇 Leicester Square 🎫 Free

ROYAL ACADEMY

Major art shows, plus the annual Summer Exhibition. Don't miss rooftop Sackler Galleries.

➕ F6 ✉ Burlington House, Piccadilly, W1 ☎ 020 7300 8000 🕐 Sat–Thu 10–6, Fri 10–10 🍴 Restaurant, café 🚇 Green Park or Piccadilly 🎫 Expensive

WALLACE COLLECTION

The Wallace Collection is the product of five generations of discerning art collectors; all members of the Hertford dynasty. They bought works by Ramsay, Canaletto, Gainsborough, Dutch 17th-century artists and quality French art. The illegitimate son of the 4th Marquess, Sir Richard Wallace, added his more treasures. The roofed courtyard has a good restaurant.

➕ E5 ✉ Hertford House, Manchester Square, W1 ☎ 020 7935 0687 🕐 Mon–Sat 10–5, Sun noon–5 🍴 All day courtyard café/restaurant 🚇 Bond Street 🎫 Free

WHITECHAPEL ART GALLERY

The hub of vibrant East End art activities, showcasing modern and contemporary works..

➕ L5 ✉ 80 Whitechapel High Street, E1 ☎ 020 7522 7888 🕐 Tue, Wed, Fri–Sun 11–5, Thu 11–9 🍴 Café 🚇 Aldgate East 🎫 Free

WINSTON CHURCHILL'S BRITAIN AT WAR EXPERIENCE

A tribute to ordinary people who lived their lives against the backdrop of air raids, the blackout, rationing and evacuation in World War II.

➕ K6 ✉ Churchill House, 64–66 Tooley Street, SE1 ☎ 020 7403 3171 🕐 Apr–end Sep daily 10–5.30; Oct–end Mar 10–4.30 🚇 London Bridge 🚉 London Bridge 🎫 Moderate

Veterans can relive 'all the fun of the war' at the Imperial War Museum in London

LONDON TRANSPORT MUSEUM

This musem tells the story of the world's largest urban public transport system, which covers more than 8000,000km (5000,000 miles). There are buttons to push and plenty of vehicles. Star attractions include the underground simulator, the touch screens in six languages, actors on the vehicles–and the shop.

➕ G5 ✉ Covent Garden Piazza, WC2 ☎ 020 7379 6344 🕐 Sat–Thu 10–6, Fri 11–6, last admission 5.15. Closed 24–26 Dec 🍴 Café 🚇 Covent Garden 🚉 Charing Cross 🎫 Moderate

53

House Museums

Dr. Johnson's House

APSLEY HOUSE (WELLINGTON MUSEUM)
Splendid mansion built for Arthur Wellesley, Duke of Wellington (1759–1852). The sumptuous interiors house his magnificent collection of paintings, silver, porcelain, sculpture and furniture.
➕ E6 ✉ Hyde Park Corner, W1 ☎ 020 7499 5676 🕐 Tue–Sun 11–5 🚇 Hyde Park Corner 💳 Moderate

CHISWICK HOUSE
Lord Burlington's exquisite country villa (1725–29), whose formal garden is an integral part of his design. Don't miss a stroll along nearby Chiswick Mall.
➕ Off map at A8 ✉ Burlington Lane, W4 ☎ 020 8995 0508 🕐 Apr–end Sep Sun–Fri 10–6, Sat 10–2; Oct Sun–Fri 10–5, Sat 10–2 🍴 Café 🚇 Turnham Green 🚉 Chiswick 💳 Moderate

DR. JOHNSON'S HOUSE
Dr. Samuel Johnson lived here between 1749 and 1759 while compiling his dictionary. The house was built c1700.
➕ H5 ✉ 17 Gough Square, EC4 ☎ 020 7353 3745 🕐 May–end Sep Mon–Sat 11–5.30; Oct–end Apr 11–5 🚇 Chancery Lane or Blackfriars 🚉 Blackfriars 💳 Moderate

HAM HOUSE
Thameside baroque mansion dating from 1610; house and garden meticulously restored.
➕ Off map at A10 ✉ Ham, Richmond, Surrey ☎ 020 8940 1950 🕐 House Apr–end Oct Sat–Wed 1–5. Gardens Sat–Wed 11–6 (or dusk) 🍴 Tearoom 🚇 Richmond, then bus 371 💳 Expensive

HANDEL HOUSE MUSEUM
Anyone who plays a muscial instrument or sings 'The Messiah' at Christmas should not miss a visit to the composer's London home from 1723 until 1759.
➕ E5 ✉ 25 Brook Street, W1 ☎ 020 7495 1685 🕐 Tue–Wed, Fri–Sat 10–6, Thu 10–8, Sun noon–6 🚇 Bond Street 💳 Moderate

SPENCER HOUSE
Lavishly restored Palladian mansion, a rare survivor of 18th-century aristocratic St. James's and Mayfair. Eight rooms featuring elegant gilded decorations, period paintings and furniture.
➕ F6 ✉ 27 St. James's Place, SW1 ☎ 020 7499 8620 🕐 Sun 10.30–5.45, Feb–end Jul, Sep–end Dec; booking advised, compulsory guided tour 🚇 Green Park 💳 Expensive; no children under 10

LEIGHTON HOUSE
Lord Leighton made his reputation when Queen Victoria bought one of his paintings. George Aitchison then designed his home-cum-studio (1861–66). The fashionable painter and esthete gave the rooms rich red walls edged with ebonized wood. Their centrepiece is the Arab Hall, one of London's most exotic rooms, lined with Persian and Saracenic blue and green tiles collected by Leighton during his travels.
➕ B7 ✉ 12 Holland Park Road, W14 ☎ 020 7602 3316 🕐 Wed–Mon 11–5.30 🚇 High Street Kensington 💳 Free

Statues & Monuments

BURGHERS OF CALAIS
Auguste Rodin's muscular bronze citizens (1915).
✚ G7 ✉ Victoria Tower Gardens, SW1 Ⓡ Westminster

CHARLES I
This superb equestrian statue of Charles I was made by Hubert Le Sueur in 1633.
✚ G6 ✉ South side of Trafalgar Square Ⓡ Charing Cross
Ⓡ Charing Cross

DUKE OF WELLINGTON
The only London hero to have three equestrian statues: The others are in St. Paul's Cathedral and outside the Duke's home, Apsley House (▶ 54).
✚ J5 ✉ Opposite the Bank of England, EC2 Ⓡ Bank

EROS
Alfred Gilbert's memorial (1893) to the philanthropic 7th Earl of Shaftesbury (1801–85) actually portrays the Angel of Christian Charity, not Eros.
✚ F5 ✉ Piccadilly Circus, W1 Ⓡ Piccadilly Circus

MONUMENT
Wren's 61.5-m (202-ft) Doric column commemorates the Great Fire (1666). Climb the 311 steps for the view.
✚ K5 ✉ Monument Street, EC3 ☎ 020 7626 2717 ⏰ Daily 10–6 Ⓡ Monument

NELSON'S COLUMN
Horatio, Viscount Nelson (1758–1805) went up on to his 52-m (172-ft) column in 1843; the hero died as he defeated the French and Spanish at Trafalgar.
✚ G6 ✉ Trafalgar Square Ⓡ Charing Cross Ⓡ Charing Cross

OLIVER CROMWELL
King-like Cromwell, Lord Protector of England from 1653 to 1658, looks across Parliament Square.
✚ G7 ✉ Houses of Parliament Ⓡ Westminster

PETER PAN
George Frampton's statue (1912) of J. M. Barrie's creation, the boy who never grew up.
✚ C6 ✉ Long Water, Kensington Gardens Ⓡ Lancaster Gate

QUEEN ALEXANDRA
This art-nouveau bronze designed by Alfred Gilbert, a memorial to Edward VII's Danish-born wife, was commissioned by her daughter-in-law, Queen Mary.
✚ F6 ✉ Marlborough Road, SW1 Ⓡ Green Park

SIR ARTHUR SULLIVAN
William Goscombe John's bronze of the operetta composer Sir Arthur Sullivan (1842–1900).
✚ G5 ✉ Embankment Gardens Ⓡ Embankment

BROADGATE CENTRE

Part of the rampant redevelopment of the City in the 1980s, Broadgate was exceptional for its commissioning of public art. *Fulcrum* by Richard Serra–vast steel sheets tentatively resting against each other–marks the Broadgate square entrance. Beyond are Barry Flanagan's *Leaping Hare on Crescent and Bell* and George Segal's *Rush Hour*. In the middle of Broadgate is the circular Arena, which becomes an outdoor ice rink in winter. Around its edge are chic restaurants, wine bars and some shops.

Peter Pan in Kensington Gardens

55

New & Renovated Buildings

30 ST. MARY AXE

Rising from the City's newest public plaza, this new 40-storey landmark tower, designed by Foster & Partners, and affectionately known as the 'gherkin', adds wit to the cluster of tall buildings in London's financial centre. It is the capital's first environmentally progressive tall buiding with its aerodynamic form encouraging wind flow around its face, which improves wind conditions in the vicinity, together with the use of natural ventilation and light, and energy saving systems.

The striking new Swiss Re headquarters designed by Foster & Partners

BRITISH LIBRARY
Colin St. John Wilson's redbrick home (1998) for the nation's books, with public galleries and piazza.
✚ G3 ✉ 96 Euston Road, NW1 ☎ 020 7412 7332 ◷ Mon–Fri 9.30–6, Tue 9.30–8, Sat 9.30–5, Sun 11–5 🍴 Café, restaurant 🚇 Kings Cross 🎫 Free; donation appreciated

BRITISH MUSEUM
Foster and Partners have created the Great Court (1998), a glass-roofed central courtyard with new amenities that make the BM perhaps the most pleasing of all national museums (➤ 45).

CANARY WHARF
César Pelli's soaring, pyramid-topped tower (1991)—the first to be clad in stainless steel—dominates Canary Wharf. The two newer towers are by Pelli and Foster.
✚ Off map at N6 ✉ 1 Canada Square, Canary Wharf, Isle of Dogs, E14 ◷ Public spaces are open, not buildings 🚇 Canary Wharf

CITY HALL
Foster and Partners designed the headquarters for the newly created Mayor of London's administration. The building's shape is to achieve maximum internal volume for minimum external surface, and leans to the south to avoid solar gain and thus control its internal temperature.
✚ J6 ✉ The Queen's Wharf, SE1 🚇 London Bridge

COUNTY HALL
A 1920s Grade II listed building on the South Bank that has been sympathetically transformed into a leisure complex including the London Aquarium (➤ 61), Dali Universe and Saatchi Gallery.
✚ G6 ✉ County Hall, Riverside Building, Westminster Bridge Road, SE1 🍴 Cafés/restaurants 🚇 Westminster

NEW THAMES BRIDGES
The Millennium Bridge links newly cleaned St. Paul's Cathedral and the City on the north bank to Tate Modern's refurbished industrustrial building on the south bank, while Lifschutz Davisdon's Hungerford Bridge connects Westminster with the South Bank cultural centre and the BA London Eye.
✚ J5; G6 🚇 stations at all ends

PORTCULLIS HOUSE
Michael Hopkins and Partners' modern defensive building for the Government, to house 210 Members of Pariliament, was designed to be terrorist proof and to last 200 years. An underground tunnel links it to the Palace of Westminster.
✚ G6 ◷ Closed to the public 🚇 Westminster

Churches & Cathedrals

In the Top 25

⛫ **HM TOWER OF LONDON** (➤ 50)
⛫ **ST. BARTHOLOMEW-THE-GREAT** (➤ 48)
⛫ **ST. PAUL'S CATHEDRAL** (➤ 46)
⛫ **WESTMINSTER ABBEY** (➤ 37)

ALL-HALLOWS-BY-THE-TOWER
Begun about 1000, the church contains a Roman pavement and a carving by Grinling Gibbons. Do not miss the Undercroft Museum.
✚ K5 ✉ Byward Street, EC3 ☎ 020 7481 2928 🕐 Church Mon–Fri 9–6, Sat–Sun 10–5 🚇 Tower Hill ✋ Charge for audio tour

HOLY TRINITY, SLOANE STREET
Late Gothic Revival church with glorious Arts and Crafts interior and glass by Burne-Jones, William Morris and others.
✚ E7 ✉ Sloane Street, SW1 ☎ 020 7730 7270 🕐 Mon–Sat 8.30–5.30, Sun 8.30–1.30 🚇 Sloane Square ✋ Donation

ORATORY OF ST. PHILIP NERI
Also known as the Brompton or London Oratory (1876). Fine baroque interior.
✚ D7 ✉ Brompton Road, SW7 ☎ 020 7808 0900 🕐 Daily 6.30am–8pm 🚇 South Kensington ✋ Donation

ST. JAMES'S, PICCADILLY
Wren's chic church (1682–84) for local aristocracy has a sumptuous interior. Superb concerts.
✚ F6 ✉ 197 Piccadilly, SW1 ☎ 020 7734 4511 🕐 Daily 8–7 🍴 Café 🚇 Piccadilly Circus ✋ Donation

ST. MARGARET, LOTHBURY
Wren's church (1686–90) retains its huge carved screen with soaring ealge and carved pulpit tester.
✚ J5 ✉ Lothubry, EC1 ☎ 020 7606 8330 🕐 Mon–Fri 7–5 🚇 Bank ✋ Donation

SOUTHWARK CATHEDRAL
Atmospheric of its medieval origins, despite much rebuilding; fine choir and monuments.
✚ J6 ✉ Montague Close, SE1 ☎ 020 7367 6700 🕐 Daily 8–6 🚇 London Bridge 🚉 London Bridge ✋ Moderate

TEMPLE CHURCH
Begun about 1160, this private chapel has a circular plan inspired by Jerusalem's Dome of the Rock. Effigies honour the Knights Templar, protectors of pilgrims to the Holy Land.
✚ H5 ✉ Inner Temple, EC4 ☎ 020 7353 3470 🕐 Wed–Sat 11–4, Sun services; occasional closure for functions 🚇 Temple ✋ Donation

CHAPELS ROYAL

London's five Chapels Royal are at St. James's Palace, Queen's Chapel, the Tower (St. Peter ad Vincula and St. John's) and Hampton Court Palace. The best services to attend are at St. Peter ad Vincula, St. James's Palace and Hampton Court, as each retains a lavish, courtly atmosphere and has a superb choir.

The Oratory of St. Philip Neri (Brompton Oratory), by Herbert Gribble (1876)

Green Spaces

London is almost 11 per cent parkland and has 174sq km (67sq miles) of green space, including the nine royal parks, former royal hunting grounds.

In the Top 25

6 HAMPSTEAD HEATH (➤ 31)
2 KENSINGTON GARDENS (➤ 27)
7 REGENT'S PARK (➤ 32)
1 ROYAL BOTANICAL GARDENS, KEW (➤ 26)
10 ST. JAMES'S PARK (➤ 35)

BUNHILL FIELDS
Leafy City oasis, where trees shade the tombs of William Blake and Daniel Defoe.
✚ J4 ✉ City Road, EC1 🕐 Daily 7.30–dusk 🚇 Old Street 💷 Free

Riders in Rotten Row, Hyde Park

GREEN PARK
Peaceful royal park.
✚ F6 ✉ SW1 ☎ 020 7930 1793 🕐 Daily dawn–dusk 🚇 Green Park or Hyde Park Corner 💷 Free

GREENWICH (➤ 20)

HOLLAND PARK
Woodland and open lawns fill 22ha (54 acres) around Holland House.
✚ A6 ✉ W8 ☎ 020 7471 9813 🕐 Daily 8–dusk 🍴 Restaurant, café 🚇 Holland Park or High Street Kensington 💷 Free

HOLY TRINITY, BROMPTON
A large, tree-shaded, airy churchyard, useful between South Kensington Museum visits.
✚ D7 ✉ Brompton Road, SW7 🕐 24 hours 🚇 South Kensington 💷 Free

HYDE PARK
One of London's largest open spaces, tamed by 18th-century royalty. Also the Serpentine Gallery (➤ 27).
✚ D6 ✉ W2 ☎ 020 7298 2100 🕐 Daily 5–midnight 🍴 Restaurant, café 🚇 Marble Arch, High Street Kensington or Hyde Park Corner 💷 Free

PRIMROSE HILL
One of London's best panoramas.
✚ D2 ✉ NW3 ☎ 020 7486 7905 🕐 Daily dawn–9pm 🚇 St. John's Wood or Camden Town 💷 Free

RUSSELL SQUARE
Lawns, trees and café near the British Museum.
✚ G4 ✉ WC1 🕐 Daily 7–dusk 🍴 Café 🚇 Russell Square 💷 Free

ROYAL PARKS

The nine royal parks, mostly former hunting grounds, are Londoners' substitute backyards. They act as the city's green lungs and many are also important bird sanctuaries. Their open spaces, woods, meadows, ponds and wide variety of mature trees have been the setting for events ranging from the Great Exhibition of 1851 to riotous demonstrations. Today, they are places to meet, picnic, play games and, in summer, enjoy a concert or a play.

Thames Sights

London grew up around the Thames. As the port expanded, so did London's wealth and power. The Thames was its main thoroughfare, used by all.

In the Top 25

🔢 **BRITISH AIRWAYS LONDON EYE (▶ 42)**
🔢 **HM THE TOWER OF LONDON (▶ 50)**
🔢 **HOUSES OF PARLIAMENT (▶ 38)**
🔢 **ROYAL BOTANICAL GARDENS, KEW (▶ 26)**
🔢 **SOMERSET HOUSE (▶ 43)**
🔢 🔢 **TATE GALLERIES (▶ 36, 47)**

SEE ALSO CITY HALL, PORTCULLIS HOUSE, NEW THAMES BRIDGES (▶ 56)

CLEOPATRA'S NEEDLE

The 26-m (86-ft) pink-granite obelisk made in 1450BC records the triumphs of Rameses the Great.
🟦 G6 ✉ Victoria Embankment, WC2 🔵 Embankment or Charing Cross 🚻 Free

DOCKLANDS

Waterparks, the high-level Docklands Light Railway, Island Gardens, Museum in Docklands and more.
✉ Stretches eastward from Tower of London to Royal Docks ⏰ 24 hours for public areas 🚇 Use DLR to explore 🚻 Free

DRAGONS ON THE EMBANKMENT

The silver cast-iron dragons (1849) mark the City of London boundary.
🟦 H5 ✉ Victoria Embankment, WC2 🔵 Temple

MILLENNIUM DOME

Richard Rogers and Partners' huge landmark dome (▶ 15) at Greenwich Peninsula remains empty, awaiting a new role. Good views from boats.
🟦 Off map at N8 ✉ Greenwich Peninsula, SE10
🚢 Riverboat to the Thames Barrier

TOWER BRIDGE EXPERIENCE

Opened in 1894; fine views from the museum and catwalk between the towers; engine rooms at the south bank end.
🟦 K6 ✉ Tower Bridge, SE1 ☎ 020 7403 3761
⏰ Daily 9.30–6; last admission 5 🔵 Tower Hill
🚢 Riverboat to Tower Pier 🚻 Moderate

WATERLOO & MILLENNIUM BRIDGES

Gilbert Scott's mid-19th century cantilevered concrete, and Caro and Rogers' 2000 superfine span (▶ 15), both with great views.
Waterloo Bridge 🟦 H6 ✉ WC2 🔵 Waterloo
Millennium Bridge 🟦 J5–J6 ✉ EC4 🔵 Mansion House

RIVERBOATS

On a sunny day, take the Underground to Westminster and catch a riverboat up or down the Thames for the morning. Trips downstream pass Westminster, the City and Docklands, stopping at several piers. A longer trip upstream meanders past London's villages, stopping at Putney Bridge, Kew, Richmond and Hampton Court piers.

The Prospect of Whitby, an old riverside smugglers' pub in Wapping

For the Family

BACKSTAGE TOURS

Going behind the scenes is great fun. In London, there are some excellent backstage tours. See how the scenery, props and costumes are made at the National Theatre (► 81), or explore backstage at Shakespear's Globe Theatre (☎ 020 7401 9919) and the Royal Opera House (► 56). Sports-keen kids can join tours of the MCC at Lord's (► 62 panel), Rugby Football Union Stadium at Twickenham (☎ 020 8892 2000) and Wimbledon Lawn Tennis Club (☎ 020 8944 1066). Reservations recommended for all.

Bethnal Green Museum of Childhood

BETHNAL GREEN MUSEUM OF CHILDHOOD

This outpost of the Victoria & Albert Museum (► 30) is an enormous train shed packed with Noah's arks, dolls, toy soldiers, puppets and even a model circus.
➕ M3 ✉ Cambridge Heath Road, E2 ☎ 020 8983 5200/2415 🕐 Sat–Thu 10–5.50 🍴 Café 🚇 Bethnal Green 🚉 Bethnal Green 💷 Free

FIREPOWER

The Royal Artillery collections in the historic Royal Arsenal, ranging from Roman trebuchets to an Iraqi supergun, plus plenty of visitor participation.
➕ Off the map from H7 ✉ The Royal Arsenal, Woolwich, SE18 ☎ 0208 8855 7755 🕐 Apr–end Oct Wed–Sun 11–5; Nov–end Mar Fri–Sun 11–5 🚉 Woolwich Arsenal ⛴ Ferry from Greenwich 💷 Expensive

GOLDEN HINDE

The exact replica of Sir Francis Drake's galleon in which he circumnavigated the globe between 1577 and 1580. The cramped interior of the ship is spread across five floors and would have been home to more than 80 sailors. Take a guided tour.
➕ J6 ✉ St. Mary Overie Dock, Cathedral Street, SE1 ☎ 0870 011 8700 🕐 Daily from around 10 until dusk, but hours vary 🚇 London Bridge 🚉 London Bridge 💷 Moderate

HAMLEYS

An everlasting favourite, a tourist attraction in its own right, and five floors packed with toys and crowds. Huge selection of board games and a video arcade in the basement. High prices.
➕ F5 ✉ 188–192 Regent Street, W1 ☎ 0870 333 2455 🕐 Mon–Sat 10–8, Sun noon–6 🚇 Oxford Circus 💷 Free

HMS *BELFAST*

Put aside two hours to clamber up, down and around this 1938 war cruiser, visiting the cabins, gun turrets, bridge and boiler-room. One of the most spectacular sights on the River Thames.
➕ K6 ✉ Morgan's Lane, Tooley Street, SE1 ☎ 020 7940 6300 🕐 Mar–end Oct daily 10–6; Nov–end Feb 10–5 🍴 Café 🚇 London Bridge 🚉 London Bridge 💷 Moderate; children under 16 free

IMAX CINEMAS

London's two gargantuan screens are at the Wellcome Wing of the Science Museum (► 29), and on the South Bank.

➕ G6 ✉ BFI London IMAX Cinema, 1 Charlie Chaplin Walk, South Bank, SE1 ☎ 020 7902 1234 🕐 Daily 1–8.30; late shows Fri, Sat 🚇 Waterloo 🚉 Waterloo 💵 Expensive

LITTLE ANGEL THEATRE

Acclaimed worldwide for its highly imaginative productions that use puppets of all sizes and shapes, this gem is magical theatre for all.

➕ H2 ✉ 14 Dagmar Passage, N1 ☎ 020 7226 1787 🕐 Shows Thu–Fri 4.30, Sat–Sun 11, 2 🚇 Angel or Highbury & Islington 💵 Moderate

LONDON AQUARIUM

An aquatic spectacular. Follow the story of a stream, an ocean, a coral reef and more.

➕ G6 ✉ County Hall, Riverside Building, Westminster Bridge Road, SE1 ☎ 020 7967 8000 🕐 Daily 10–6 🚇 Westminster 💵 Expensive

MADAME TUSSAUD'S & THE LONDON PLANETARIUM

Madame Tussaud learned the art of waxworks from her uncle; see how many people you can identify, from Shakespeare to Madonna, and do not miss the Spirit of London ride. The Planetarium has good star shows and an interactive exhibition area.

➕ E4 ✉ Marylebone Road, W1 ☎ 0870 400 3000 🕐 Daily 9.30–5.30. Planetarium shows run every 20 mins Mon–Fri 12.30–5, Sat–Sun 10.30–5 🍴 Café 🚇 Baker Street 💵 Expensive; family ticket; Tussaud's/Planetarium combined ticket

THE ORIGINAL LONDON SIGHTSEEING TOUR

Cruise about town on an open-top double-decker bus whose four routes cover 90 stops; tickets and route maps available on board.

➕ Moves around central London ✉ Pick-up points include Victoria Street, Marble Arch, Baker Street, Embankment Pier, Park Lane ☎ 020 8877 1722 🕐 Daily 9–7 in summer, 9–5.30 in winter; departures every 15–20 mins approximately 💵 Expensive. Ticket valid 24 hours

TOY WORLD, HARRODS

Up on the fourth floor, this is every child's dream outing. Plenty of toys for children to play with.

➕ D7 ✉ Brompton Road, SW1 ☎ 020 7730 1234 🕐 Mon–Sat 10–7 🍴 Restaurants, cafés 🚇 Knightsbridge 💵 Free

WWT WETLAND CENTRE

The well-established Wildfowl and Wetlands Trust administer 42ha (104 acres) of lakes, ponds, grassland and mudflats that attract an abundance of wildlife.

➕ Off the map to southwest ✉ Queen Elizabeth's Walk, SW13 ☎ 020 8409 4400 🕐 Mar–end Oct daily 9.30–6; Nov–end Feb 9.30–5 (last admission 1 hour before closing) 🚇 Hammersmith, then bus 283 🚉 Barnes then bus 33, 72 💵 Expensive

Harrods—an outing in itself

LONDON FOR FREE

London has plenty of free activities for all ages. Several public galleries are free (National Gallery ➤ 41, National Portrait Gallery ➤ 40, Tate Galleries, free except for special exhibitions ➤ 36, 47) plus the commercial ones (➤ 75). Many museums are free and music can be enjoyed in church concerts, pubs and arts complexes. For free theatre, try an art auction (➤ 75), a debate in Parliament (➤ 38) or a BBC recording session (☎ 020 8743 8000 and ask for ticket inquiries, specifying radio or TV).

61

Hidden London

In the Top 25
14 BANQUETING HOUSE (➤ 39)

CRICKET

Anyone who watches or plays cricket should visit the MCC Museum hidden away at Lord's. The story of the game is told in pictures, cartoons and old battered bats; the Ashes are kept here, too. It is open to ticket-holders on match days, while at other times the guided tour includes the Long Room and the beautiful new stand designed by Michael Hopkins in 1985–87.
➕ D3 ✉ Marylebone Cricket Club, Lord's Ground, NW8 ☎ 020 7432 1033. Tour bookings 020 7616 8595/6 🕐 Guided tours phone for availability 🚇 St. John's Wood 🎟 Expensive

CHELSEA PHYSIC GARDEN

Sir Hans Sloane laid out this walled garden for the Society of Apothecaries in 1673.
➕ D8 ✉ 66 Royal Hospital Road, SW3 ☎ 020 7352 5646 🕐 Apr–end Oct Wed noon–5, Sun 2–6 🚇 Sloane Square 🎟 Moderate

CLARENCE HOUSE

Built for Prince William, Duke of Clarence and later William IV, this was the Queen Mother's London home, now renovated by the new resident, The Prince of Wales. All tickets are timed and must be pre-booked.
➕ F6 ✉ Off The Mall, SW1 ☎ 020 7766 7303 🕐 Mid–Aug to end Oct daily 9–7 🚇 St. James's Park or Green Park 🎟 Moderate

HIDDEN LONDON WALKS

The Original London Walks Company, based in north London, take a wide range of walks including Secret London, Hidden London and trails exploring the lesser known-areas of the city.
➕ Moves around central London ☎ 020 7624 3978; recorded information 020 7624 9255; www.walks.com 🕐 Variable 🎟 Moderate

ROYAL HOSPITAL, CHELSEA

Wren's 1682 building, inspired by the Hôtel des Invalides in Paris, is still a home for veteran soldiers. Look out for the gilded Charles II in the grounds.
➕ E8 ✉ Royal Hospital Road, SW3 ☎ 020 7881 5466 🕐 Museum, Great Hall, Chapel Mon–Fri 10–noon, 2–4, Sat 2–4 (also Sun 2–4, May–end Sep; Sun service 10.40). Closed 15 May to end Jun and public hols 🚇 Sloane Square 🎟 Free

VINOPOLIS

A warren of atmospheric rooms devoted to the world's wine-growing regions, with films, experts and plenty of tastings.
➕ J6 ✉ 1 Bank End, SE1 ☎ 0870 241 4040 🕐 Tue–Thu & Sun noon–6, Mon, Fri–Sat noon–9; last admission 2 hours before closing 🚇 London Bridge 🚆 London Bridge 🎟 Expensive, includes audio-guide and tastings

2 WILLOW ROAD

Designer Erno Goldfinger's striking home, built in 1939, complete with its contents. Guided tours only.
➕ Off the map ✉ 22 Willow Road, NW3 ☎ 020 7435 6166 🕐 Apr–Oct Thu–Sat noon–5; Mar, Nov Sat only noon–5 🚇 Hampstead 🎟 Moderate

Chelsea Pensioners, residents of the Royal Hospital, Chelsea

LONDON
where to...

British & Modern Restaurants

PRICES

Eating out in London is generally expensive and prices vary widely. In the restaurants listed on these pages, expect to pay per person for a meal (including drinks):

£ under £30
££ £30–£60
£££ more than £60

When the bill (check) arrives, look it over carefully as a service charge (usually 10–12½ per cent) and sometimes cover charges (approximately £2 per person) may be added. Check beforehand whether VAT and coffee are also included, and order tap water if you do not want to pay for bottled. A good-value menu can be transformed into an outrageous bill if you do not look sharp. You are not obliged to leave a tip if service is added even if the credit card slip is left open.

BRITISH CUISINE

British cuisine should no longer be derided; there is both fine traditional and impressive new wave cooking to be enjoyed.

THE GLASSHOUSE (££)

The perfect preamble to a walk in Kew Gardens (► 26). Reserve to enjoy notable modern dishes right beside Kew station.
Off the map from A8 14 Station Parade, Kew 020 8940 6777 Lunch, dinner Kew Gardens

GORING HOTEL (££)

The style is classic country houe; the cooking traditional British with modern touches.
F7 15 Beeston Place, SW1 020 7396 9000 Sun–Fri lunch, dinner Victoria

INN THE PARK (££)

What London has long needed; a good restaurant in an interesting new building set in one of the royal parks, and stylish British food with especially good cheeses.
F6 St. James's Park, SW1 020 7451 9999 Lunch, dinner St. James's Park

THE IVY (£££)

A revived theatreland classic with artworks by Peter Blake and Howard Hodgkin on the walls, celebrities galore and modern European food.
G5 1 West Street, WC2 020 7836 4751 Lunch, dinner Leicester Square

LAUNCESTON PLACE RESTAURANT (££)

Discreetly tucked away in a corner of South Kensington—excellent modern British cooking despite its genial old fashioned atmosphere.
C7 1a Launceston Place, W8 020 7937 6912 Sun–Fri lunch, Mon–Sat dinner Gloucester Road

MEDCALF (£)

Informal, with music at night, yet a carefully crafted menu that respects top quality ingredients; good desserts, too.
H4 40 Exmouth Markert, EC1 020 7833 3533 Mon–Fri, Sun lunch, dinner, Sat dinner Farringdon

RULES (££)

One of London's oldest restaurants, founded in 1798, serves good traditional English dishes in plush Edwardian rooms.
G5 35 Maiden Lane, WC2 020 7836 5314 Lunch, dinner Covent Garden

ST. JOHN (££)

Robust dishes ranging from rabbit to oxtails to serious puddings. Plenty of offal.
H4 26 St. John Street, EC1 020 7251 0848 Mon–Fri lunch, Mon–Sat dinner. Closed Sun Farringdon

TOP FLOOR AT SMITHS (££)

Excellent steaks, organic and additive-free produce with Dickensian views. In summer eat alfresco.
H4 66–67 Chaterhouse Street, EC1 020 7251 7950 Mon–Fri lunch, Mon–Sat dinner Farringdon

THE WOLSELEY (££)

Jeremy King and Chris Corbin, who made the Ivy an institution, are repeating their success in a splendid former bank and car showroom; eat modern European dishes modestly or grandly.
F6 160 Piccadilly, W1 020 7499 6996 Lunch, dinner Farringdon

Italian & French Restaurants

THE ADMIRALTY (££)
Oliver Peyton's restaurant empire grows with this stunning site, serving modern continental dishes.
➕ H5 ✉ Somerset House, WC2 ☎ 020 7845 4646 🕐 Lunch, Mon–Sat dinner Ⓜ Temple

ALMEIDA (££)
Undaunted by the plethora of restaurants in Islington, Conran has arrived with this very French, pleasingly unostentatious success.
➕ H2 ✉ 30 Almeida Street, N1 ☎ 020 7354 4777 🕐 Lunch, dinner Ⓜ Angel or Highbury & Islington

AL SAN VINCENZO (££)
It is essential to reserve a table to enjoy Neapolitan Signore Borgonzolo's cooking.
➕ D5 ✉ 30 Connaught Street, W2 ☎ 020 7262 9623 🕐 Mon–Fri lunch, Mon–Sat dinner Ⓜ Marble Arch

ASSAGGI (££)
Popular Italian above the Chepstow pub specializing in a dozen or so starters called *assaggi* (little tastes). Reserve well in advance.
➕ B5 ✉ The Chepstow, 39 Chepstow Place, W2 ☎ 020 7792 5501 🕐 Mon–Fri lunch, Mon–Sat dinner Ⓜ Westbourne Park

CAFÉ DU MARCHÉ (££)
In the cobblestone mews in the square's west corner, this rustic French restaurant has a laid-back pianist each evening.
➕ J4 ✉ 22 Charterhouse Square, EC1 ☎ 020 7608 1609 🕐 Mon–Fri lunch, Mon–Sat dinner Ⓜ Barbican

CLUB GASCON (££)
Unusual, robust dishes from Gascony; good for City or post-Barbican Centre dinner. Reserve well in advance.
➕ J4 ✉ 57 West Smithfield, EC1 ☎ 020 7796 0600 🕐 Mon–Fri lunch, Mon–Sat dinner Ⓜ Barbican or Farringdon

PEIDÁ TERRE (££)
Good value, given that the reward is a thoroughly spoiling French gourmet experience; worth taking the set-price menu.
➕ F4 ✉ 34 Charlotte Street, W1 ☎ 020 7636 1178 🕐 Tue–Fri lunch, Mon–Sat dinner Ⓜ Goodge Street

PLATEAU (£££)
Ideally matched to its sleek surroundings, this Conran bar, grill and restaurant has much glass, a lush terrace, French food and fine 4th-floor views.
➕ Off map at N5 ✉ Canada Place, Canada Square, Canary Wharf, E14 ☎ 020 7715 7100 🕐 Lunch, Mon–Sat dinner Ⓜ Canary Wharf

SARDO (££)
Patrons come for Romolo Mudo's Sardinian dishes; well worth chatting to him for ideas before you order.
➕ F5 ✉ 45 Grafton Way, W1 ☎ 020 7387 2521 🕐 Mon–Fri lunch, Mon–Sat dinner Ⓜ Warren Street

TOM AITKINS (££)
Delicious haute cuisine and superb service to be enjoyed in a fresh, contemporary setting. Good value set-price menu.
➕ D7 ✉ 43 Elystan Street, SW3 ☎ 020 7584 2003 🕐 Lunch, Mon–Fri dinner Ⓜ South Kensington

SET-PRICE MENUS
Many of London's pricier restaurants offer two set-price menus serving sublime dishes–lower in price at lunchtime. Consider dressing up to try classic Anglo-French cuisine at the exquisite Connaught Grill (➕ E5 ✉ 16 Carlos Place, W1 ☎ 020 7499 7070) or spend an afternoon lunching at Gordon Ramsey's restaurant (► 68). Most of the star chefs offer these menus including Richard Corrigan and Philip Howard (► 68).

Asian Restaurants

INDIAN FOOD

London's 2,000 or so Indian restaurants cater to a well-informed local clientele, so this is a good moment to visit one. An Indian meal should have many dishes so, if you are a group, consider making a collective order and sharing. Tandoori dishes (cooked in a clay oven) make good starters. Main course dishes should arrive together and include one or two meat offerings, two or three vegetable dishes, rice, a lentil or pulse serving (such as chickpeas), and a variety of breads such as *chapati* or *naan*–which are eaten hot, so order more as you go along. Remember the yoghurt and pickles, and drink *lassi* (sweet or salty variations on buttermilk/yoghurt) or beer. Vegetarians will find a good range of mild and spicy food.

BENARAS (££)

Atul Kochhar, ex-Tamarind restaurant, serves up serious Indian dishes including little-known receipes from his native Uttar Pradesh. If confused, have a set menu.
♦ F6 ⊠ 12 Berkeley House, Berkeley Square, W1 ☎ 020 7629 8886 ⏰ Mon–Fri lunch, Mon–Sat dinner 🚇 Green Park

IKKYU (£)

Efficiently served and very notable Japanese food at impressively fair prices; the *tempura* is especially good here.
♦ F4 ⊠ 67 Tottenham Court Road, W1 ☎ 020 7636 9280 ⏰ Mon–Fri lunch, Sun–Fri dinner 🚇 Goodge Street or Tottenham Court Road

MASALA ZONE (£)

From the creators of Chutney Mary and Veeraswamy, both loved for their authentic dishes, comes an informal setting for the distinctive Gujarati meals of western India. Branch in Islington.
♦ F5 ⊠ 9 Marshall Street, W1 ☎ 020 7287 9966 ⏰ Sun–Fri lunch, dinner 🚇 Oxford Circus

NOBU (£££)

New York's Nobuyuki Matsuhisa brings his pan-American Japanese cooking to London. Equally pricey outpost Ubon, at Canary Wharf.
♦ E6 ⊠ Metropolitan Hotel, 19 Old Park Lane, W1 ☎ 020 7447 4747 ⏰ Lunch, dinner 🚇 Hyde Park Corner

THE PAINTED HERON (££)

Yogeth Datta takes his Indian heritage, mixes in his European experiences and a dollop of imagination and comes up with delicious originals.
♦ C9 ⊠ 112 Cheyne Walk, SW10 ☎ 020 7351 5232 ⏰ Mon–Fri lunch, Mon–Sat dinner 🚇 Sloane Square or South Kensington then bus

RASA (£)

Inspired Keralan cooking, one of India's softer styles. Several siblings include Rasa Samudra.
♦ E5 ⊠ 6 Dering Street, W1 ☎ 020 7629 1346 ⏰ Lunch, Mon–Sat dinner 🚇 Bond Street

ROYAL CHINA (££)

Reserve a table or join the justifiably long lines for the best dim sum in town. Three branches.
♦ C5 ⊠ 13 Queensway, W2 ☎ 020 7221 2535 ⏰ Lunch, dinner 🚇 Queensway

SALLOOS (££)

Consistently perfect Pakistani dishes from the North-Western Frontier, ideal for meat lovers.
♦ E7 ⊠ 62–64 Kinnerton Street, SW1 ☎ 020 7235 4444 ⏰ Mon–Sat lunch, dinner 🚇 Knightsbridge

TAMARIND (££)

Delicious traditional village dishes from Uttar Prades, Kerala and other Indian states.
♦ E6 ⊠ 20 Queen Street, W1 ☎ 020 7629 3561 ⏰ Sun–Fri lunch, dinner 🚇 Green Park

WAGAMAMA (£)

Trendy Japanese *ramen* bar near the British Museum. About 20 branches; no reservations.
♦ G5 ⊠ 4a Streatham Street, WC1 ☎ 020 7323 9223 ⏰ Lunch, dinner 🚇 Tottenham Court Road

Fish & Vegetarian Restaurants

BACK TO BASICS (££)

Modestly priced, imaginative fish dishes in an unpretentious bistro a short walk from the British Museum or Oxford Street.

✚ F4 ✉ 21a Foley Street, W1 ☎ 020 7436 2181 🕐 Lunch, Mon–Sat dinner Ⓜ Goodge Street

BANK ALDWYCH (££)

Dramatic modern brasserie setting for excellent fish dishes, from 'fish and chips' to lobster.

✚ G5 ✉ 1 Kingsway, WC2 ☎ 020 7379 9797 🕐 Breakfast, lunch, dinner Ⓜ Holborn

CARNEVALE (£)

Inventive vegetarian dishes at this cramped Clerkenwell restaurant, ideal post City sight-seeing or pre-Barbican.

✚ J4 ✉ 135 Whitecross Street, EC1 ☎ 020 7250 3452 🕐 Mon–Fri lunch, Mon–Sat dinner Ⓜ Old Street

THE GATE (£)

Imaginative vegetarian food and an often-changing menu mean reserving is essential at this useful pre-show Hammersmith hideaway.

✚ Off the map from A7 ✉ 51 Queen Caroline Street, W6 ☎ 020 8748 6932 🕐 Mon–Fri lunch, Mon–Sat dinner Ⓜ Hammersmith

LIVEBAIT (££)

From its original near the Young and Old Vic theatres in The Cut, success has spawned Livebait fish restaurants across the city.

✚ H6 ✉ 43 The Cut, SE1 ☎ 020 7928 7211 🕐 Lunch, dinner Ⓜ Southwark

THE PLACE BELOW (£)

Exceptional vegetarian food in an ancient Norman church crypt in the heart of the City.

✚ J5 ✉ St. Mary-le-Bow, Cheapside, EC2 ☎ 020 7329 0789 🕐 Mon–Fri breakfast lunch Ⓜ Monument

MORGAN M (££)

Morgan Meunier, formerly of Admiralty, creates uplifting French vegetarian dishes plus memorable fish ones; reservations essential despite its fringe location.

✚ H2 ✉ 489 Liverpool Road, N7 ☎ 020 7609 3560 🕐 Wed–Fri, Sun lunch, Tue–Sat dinner Ⓜ Highbury & Islington

J. SHEEKEY (££)

Renovated and re-invigorated by The Ivy/ Caprice team, with its traditional fish dishes correspondingly refined.

✚ G5 ✉ 28–32 St. Martin's Court, WC2 ☎ 020 7240 2565 🕐 Lunch, dinner Ⓜ Leicester Square

SWEETINGS (££)

Unashamedly old-fashioned City fish parlour; no reservations, so arrive early or late if you want a table.

✚ J5 ✉ 39 Queen Victoria Street, EC4 ☎ 020 7248 3062 🕐 Mon–Fri lunch Ⓜ Mansion House

WORLD FOOD CAFÉ (£)

A fresh, modern approach to vegetarian food, featuring Indian, Mexican, Greek and Turkish influences.

✚ G5 ✉ 14 Neal's Yard, WC2 ☎ 020 7379 0298 🕐 Mon–Fri 11.30–4.30, Sat 11.30–5 Ⓜ Covent Garden

ROMANTIC EATING

If it is the setting that is important for your 'dinner a deux', consider going traditional and grand at The Ritz (✉ 150 Piccadilly, W1 ☎ 020 7493 8181). For something more dramatic and modern, the Oxo Tower's restaurant or brasserie (✉ Barge House Street, SE1 ☎ 020 7803 3888), or the top floor of the Tate Modern (✉ Bankside, SE1 ☎ 020 7401 5020) might be right; both have fantastic views. If the French atmosphere is essential, try the intimate and fairly modest La Poule au Pot (✉ 231 Ebury Street, SW1 ☎ 020 7730 7763), or perhaps Julie's (✉ 135 Portland Road, W11 ☎ 020 7229 8331). Match romance with modern British cooking at the sumptuous Launceston Place (✉ 1a Launceston Place, W8 ☎ 020 7937 6912), the spoiling Odette's (✉ 130 Regent Park Road, NW1 ☎ 020 7586 5486) or the more clubby and high fashion Le Caprice (✉ Arlington House, Arlington Street, SW1 ☎ 020 7629 2239).

VEGETARIAN EATING

Vegetarians are well catered for in London. Most restaurants offer a range of non-meat and non-fish meals, while Indian cooking is famed for its imaginative vegetable and pulse dishes. If fish remains an option, the capital has a wide range on offer.

Famous Chefs

RICHARD CORRIGAN: LINDSAY HOUSE (£££)

Inspired modern British cooking in a delightful Soho townhouse.

🔲 G5 ✉ 21 Romilly Street, W1 ☎ 020 7439 0450
🕐 Mon–Fri lunch, Mon–Sat dinner
🚇 Leicester Square

PHILIP HOWARD: THE SQUARE (£££)

Impressive modern French food matched by a chic, but formal Mayfair interior.

🔲 F5 ✉ 6 Bruton Street, W1 ☎ 020 7495 7100 🕐 Mon–Fri lunch, Mon–Sat dinner 🚇 Bond Street

JAMIE OLIVER: FIFTEEN (£££)

Always busy, this rather highly-priced eaterie is the latest of Oliver's enterprises. Mainly Italian cusine; good flavours.

🔲 J3 ✉ 15 Westland Place, N1 ☎ 0871 330 1515 🕐 Mon–Sat lunch, dinner 🚇 Old Street

BRUCE POOLE: CHEZ BRUCE (££)

Worth the journey to Wandsworth Common to enjoy Poole's interesting menu offering mainly French but also other European influences. Well-balanced flavours.

🔲 Off the map from E10 ✉ 2 Bellevue Road, SW17 ☎ 020 8672 0114 🕐 Lunch, dinner 🚇 Balham 🚉 Wandsworth Common

GORDON RAMSAY: RESTAURANT GORDON RAMSAY (£££)

A stunning interpretation of French cooking; every detail of food, service and the formal setting is perfect.

🔲 E8 ✉ 68 Royal Hospital Road, SW3 ☎ 020 7352 4441
🕐 Lunch, Mon–Fri dinner
🚇 Sloane Square

GARY RHODES: RHODES TWENTY FOUR (£££)

Gary Rhodes gives patrons the ulitmate City experience: fine British food and amazing City views enjoyed from the 24th floor of the former Nat West tower.

🔲 K5 ✉ 24th floor, Tower 42, Old Broad Street, EC2 ☎ 020 7877 7703 🕐 Mon–Fri lunch, dinner 🚇 Liverpool Street

MICHEL ROUX: LA GAVROCHE (£££)

Albert's son sticks to classic French, but lighter; amazing wines, grand setting.

🔲 E5 ✉ 43 Upper Brook Street, W1 ☎ 020 7408 0881
🕐 Mon–Fri lunch, Mon–Sat dinner 🚇 Marble Arch

BJORN VAN DER HORST: GREENHOUSE (£££)

Imaginative yet serious food (fois gras flavoured with espresso syrup and amaretto froth) by Bjorn van der Horst who made his name in New York.

🔲 F5 ✉ 27a Hay's Mews, W1 ☎ 020 7499 3331 🕐 Mon–Fri lunch, Mon–Sat dinner 🚇 Green Park

ANTHONY WORRALL THOMPSON: NOTTING GRILL (£–££)

Good range of prices here from organic bangers and mash to great steaks.

🔲 E5 ✉ 123a Clarendon Road, W11 ☎ 020 7229 1500
🕐 Sat, Sun lunch, dinner
🚇 Bond Street

RIVERSIDE EATING

London is exploiting the potential of its riverside views. Today, there is more than just the Admirality (➤ 65) and the East End smugglers' pubs. The most spectacular views are from the Oxo Tower Restaurant (➤ panel, 67) with its serious food– and prices–as well as Tate Modern's rooftop restaurant at Bankside (➤ 47). There are lower but impressive views from the second-floor Blue Print Café (☎ 020 7378 7031) beside the Design Museum, Butler's Wharf, overlooking Tower Bridge and the City (➤ 52). For more modest river-view eating, try Barley Mow pub (✉ 44 Narrow Street, E14), whose outdoor tables overlook the wider, curving Thames of the East End.

Breakfast & Tea

BANK ALDWYCH (£)

Great setting and superb breakfast to start a busy City or sightseeing day.

🔢 G5 ✉ 1 Kingsway, WC2 ☎ 020 7379 9797 🕐 Mon–Fri 7.30–10.30am 🚇 Holborn

CLARIDGE'S (£)

Breakfast is in the immaculate art-deco restaurant; tea—among the best in London—is taken on sofas in the lobby alcove. Reservations essential. Dress code: jacket and tie.

🔢 E5 ✉ Brook Street, W1 ☎ 020 7629 8860 🕐 Breakfast, tea 🚇 Bond Street

INN THE PARK (£)

Michael Hopkins designed the wooden restaurant with sweeping lawns (► 64), ideal for coffee and crissants overlooking this year-round beautiful royal park.

🔢 F6 ✉ St. James's Park, SW1 ☎ 020 7451 9999 🕐 Breakfast 🚇 St. James's Park

KONDITOR & COOK (£)

Top quality breads, savory tarts, soups and irresistible cakes—especially chocolate ones. Fortunately there are several branches.

🔢 J6 ✉ 10 Stoney Street, SE1 ☎ 020 7407 5100 🕐 Mon–Fri breakfast, tea; Sat closes 4pm 🚇 London Bridge

MANDARIN ORIENTAL HYDE PARK (££)

The window tables in the lounge conservatory overlooking Hyde Park are the best for afternoon tea.

🔢 E6 ✉ Knightsbridge, SW1 ☎ 020 7235 2000 🕐 Breakfast, tea 🚇 Hyde Park Corner

PÂTISSERIE VALERIE (£)

Coffee, croissants and delicious cakes at tiny tables in the original café-shop. Branches.

🔢 F5 ✉ 44 Old Compton Street, W1 ☎ 020 7437 3466 🕐 Breakfast, tea 🚇 Leicester Square or Tottenham Court Road

PAUL (£)

Stunning patisserie, a branch of its French mother founded in 1889; divine hot chocolate, pastries and savouries. Marylebone branch.

🔢 G5 ✉ 29 Bedford Street, WC2 ☎ 020 7836 3304 🕐 7.30am–9pm 🚇 Covent Garden

SIMPSON'S (££)

Glorious setting for a traditional breakfast, such as porridge followed by kippers or kidneys. Jacket and tie.

🔢 G5 ✉ 100 Strand, WC2 ☎ 020 7836 9112 🕐 Mon–Fri 7.15am–10.30pm 🚇 Charing Cross

VILLANDRY (£)

A perfect place to pause before or after braving the Oxford Street stores—indulge in the renowned pastries or fruit tarts.

🔢 F4 ✉ 170 Great Portland Street, W1 ☎ 020 7631 3131 🕐 Mon–Fri 8am–11pm, Sat 9–9 🚇 Great Portland Street

THE WOLSELEY (£)

Start the day in art-deco grandeur (► 65), or relax here after visiting the Royal Academy with dainty sandwiches and French cakes.

🔢 F6 ✉ 106 Piccadilly, W1 ☎ 020 7499 6996 🕐 Breakfast, tea 🚇 Green Park

BEST SETTINGS

If part of the pleasure of dining out is the setting try lunch or dinner at the Ritz (► 86) or perhaps the Coq d'Argent (✉ 1 Poultry, EC3 ☎ 020 7395 5000); the Tate Modern rooftop (► 47); the National Portrait Gallery (► 40); or the British Museum's Court Restaurant (► 45, 56). Go to the mosaic-clad Criterion (✉ 224 Piccadilly, W1 ☎ 020 7930 0488) for sparkle and Claridge's (► this page, 86) for Art Deco. Wacky settings include the Dorchester's pricey Oriental (✉ Park Lane, W1 ☎ 020 7407 2056). For atmospheric pubs go to the George Inn (✉ 77 Borough High Street, SE1) or the Admiral Codrington (► 71). For the ultimate City views, Rhodes Twenty Four (► 68) and you'll find the most beautiful walls at Christopher's (► 70). For a fabulous garden setting try the Brew House restaurant, Kenwood House (► 31) or Inn The Park in St. James's Park (► 64).

Brasseries & Brunch

THE AMERICAN EXPERIENCE

America's fast food arrived long before its quality cuisine and restaurant style became established. Upscale options include Joe Allen and Christopher's (both this page), and PJ's (⊠ 52 Fulham Road, SW3 ☎ 020 7581 0025). Other good-value places to hang out include:

Arkansas Café ⊠ Unit 12, Old Spitalfield Market, E1 ☎ 020 7377 6999

Big Easy ⊠ 1332–334 King's Road, SW3 ☎ 020 7352 4071

Eagle Ben Diner ⊠ 3–5 Rathbone Place, W1 ☎ 020 7637 1418

The Hard Rock Café ⊠ 150 Old Park Lane, W1 ☎ 020 7629 0382

Santa Fe ⊠ 75 Upper Street, N1 ☎ 020 7288 2288

BRASSERIE DE MALMAISON (££)

Sleek modern brasserie inside a Victorian building well placed for the City and the Barbican Centre.
✚ J4 ⊠ Malmaison Hotel, 18–21 Charterhouse Square, EC1 ☎ 020 70123700
🕐 Mon–Sat lunch, dinner
🚇 Barbican or Farringdon

LA BRASSERIE ST. QUENTIN (££)

Uncompromisingly French—great for an indulgent break from South Ken museums.
✚ D7 ⊠ 243 Brompton Road, SW3 ☎ 020 7589 8005
🕐 Lunch, dinner 🚇 South Kensington

CAFÉ BOHÈME (£)

Good value (*prix fixe*) and good Soho atmosphere, with a French authenticity that means even a simple omlette is delicious.
✚ F5 ⊠ 13 Old Compton Street, W1 ☎ 020 7734 0623
🕐 Lunch, dinner 🚇 Leicester Square

CAFÉ DES AMIS (££)

Good value *prix-fixe* menu and efficient service in this quiet retreat between Long Acre and the Royal Opera House.
✚ G5 ⊠ 211–14 Hanover Place, WC2 ☎ 020 7379 3444
🕐 Lunch, Mon–Sat dinner
🚇 Covent Garden

CHRISTOPHER'S (£££)

One of London's best for a genuine American brunch, and in one of the most beautiful dining rooms.
✚ G5 ⊠ 18 Wellington Street, WC2 ☎ 020 7240 4222
🕐 Lunch, Mon–Sat dinner, Sat–Sun brunch 🚇 Covent Garden

FLANEUR FOOD HALL (££)

Witty interior design in a spacious converted warehouse. Modern Mediterranean food composed with super-fresh ingredients.
✚ H4 ⊠ 41 Farringdon Road, EC1 ☎ 020 7404 4422
🕐 Lunch, Mon–Sat dinner
🚇 Farringdon

JOE ALLEN (££)

Dependably convivial and club-like. Healthy American Cal-Ital food. Reservations essential.
✚ G5 ⊠ 13 Exeter Street, WC2 ☎ 020 7836 0651
🕐 Lunch, dinner, Sat–Sun brunch 🚇 Covent Garden

JUST THE BRIDGE (££)

Stunning views of the Millennium Bridge and Tate Modern, enjoyed with modern British food.
✚ J5 ⊠ 1 Paul's Walk, EC4 ☎ 020 7236 0000 🕐 Lunch, dinner (closed Sat–Sun Oct–Easter) 🚇 Mansion House

NOTTING HILL BRASSERIE (££)

Just the place to recover after visiting Portobello Road while enjoying Mark Jankel's good food. Be sure to reserve a table.
✚ A5 ⊠ 92 Kensington Park Road, W11 ☎ 020 7229 4481
🕐 Lunch, Mon–Sat dinner
🚇 Notting Hill Gate

VINCENT ROOMS (£)

Culinary students test their skills in cooking, which are usually pretty good even at this stage.
✚ F7 ⊠ Westminster Kingsway College, Vincent Square, SW1 ☎ 020 7802 8391 🕐 Lunch Mon–Fri, phone for dinner times 🚇 Victoria or St. James's Park

Shops & Gastropubs

COACH & HORSES (££)

Outstanding food—especially the fish dishes such as organic salmon—in a modern pub setting. Good wine list and, in summer, outdoor tables.

🗗 H4 ⊠ 26–28 Ray Street, EC1 ☎ 020 7278 8990 🕐 Sun–Fri lunch, Mon–Sat dinner 🚇 Farringdon

THE EAGLE (£)

The original London new-wave pub (1991) serves robust, Mediterranean food to a noisy, full house.

🗗 H4 ⊠ 159 Farringdon Road, EC1 ☎ 020 7837 1353 🕐 Lunch, Mon–Sat dinner 🚇 Farringdon

EASTON (£)

Authentic atmosphere matched by a friendly staff, plenty of regulars and good food make this an ideal stop after, say Bloomsbury or Holborn sightseeing.

🗗 H4 ⊠ 22 Easton Street, WC1 ☎ 020 7278 7608 🕐 Lunch, dinner 🚇 Farringdon

THE ENGINEER (££)

Vibrant Primrose Hill pub with walled garden, ideal after Regent's Park, zoo or Camden markets.

🗗 E2 ⊠ 654 Gloucester Avenue, NW1 ☎ 020 7722 0950 🕐 Lunch, dinner 🚇 Chalk Farm

FIFTH FLOOR AT HARVEY NICHOLS (£££)

Modern British cuisine for a chic clientele in Julian Wickham's designer room. As an alternative, try the *Fountain* in the basement.

🗗 E6 ⊠ Knightsbridge, SW1 ☎ 020 7235 5250 🕐 Lunch, Mon–Sat dinner 🚇 Knightsbridge

HARRODS (£–££)

You're spoilt for choice here. Favourites include the Champagne and Oyster Bar and the Ice-cream Parlour.

🗗 D7 ⊠ Knightsbridge, SW1 ☎ 020 7730 1234 🕐 Breakfast, lunch, tea 🚇 Knightsbridge

NICOLE'S (££)

Figure-conscious designer food in the basement of Nicole Farhi's shop in Mayfair's luxury shopping area; handy for Sotheby's and the Royal Academy.

🗗 F5 ⊠ 158 New Bond Street, W1 ☎ 020 7499 8408 🕐 Mon–Sat lunch, Mon–Fri dinner 🚇 Bond Street

PEASANT (£)

Excellent innovative Mediterranean food in a pub touched with the wand of a design-conscious foodie.

🗗 H4 ⊠ 240 St. John Street, EC1 ☎ 020 7336 7726 🕐 Mon–Fri lunch, Mon–Sat dinner 🚇 Farringdon

SOTHEBY'S CAFÉ (££)

The lobby of this auction house is great for a light lunch—reservations are essential—or afternoon tea.

🗗 B7 ⊠ 34 Bond Street, W1 ☎ 020 7293 5077 🕐 Mon–Fri breakfast, lunch, tea 🚇 Bond Street

THE WELLS (£–££)

Choose from the cheaper ground floor or more expensive first floor at this ideal spot while spending the day in and around Hampstead. Best to reserve ahead.

🗗 Off map at C1 ⊠ 30 Well Walk, NW3 ☎ 020 7794 3785 🕐 Lunch, dinner 🚇 Hampstead

MUSEUM RESTAURANTS

Hugely improved, it is now possible to mix quality culture with quality eating at a number of London's museums. Try the Tate Britain (➤ 36), Tate Modern (➤ 47), British Museum (➤ 45, 56), National Portrait Gallery (➤ 40), Wallace Collection (➤ 53), Dulwich Picture Gallery (➤ 52), Geffrye Museum (➤ 52), National Gallery (➤ 41) and Somerset House (➤ 43). The Royal Academy's restaurant is decorated by Academicians (➤ 53). Kensington Palace's magnificent Orangery (➤ 27) offers the ultimate tea.

EAT AS MUCH AS YOU CAN BUFFET DEALS

Unlimited food at a fixed price is practical for families with growing children—or simply for hungry adults. Many larger hotels do breakfast and lunch buffets, especially good on Sundays when many Indian restaurants do the same—the Contad Hotel's luxurious buffet is legendary.

Shopping Areas

OPENING TIMES

Regular shop hours are 9.30 or 10am until between 5.30 and 7pm, with late-night shopping in Knightsbridge on Wednesdays and Oxford Street, Regent Street and Covent Garden on Thursdays.
London's stores tend to be found in clusters; conserve your energy and shop in one area.

TAX-FREE GOODS

If you are a non-EU passport holder, consider the VAT Retails Export Scheme. VAT (Value Added Tax) is rated at 17½ per cent in Britain and payable on almost everything except books, food and children's clothes. All non-EU passport holders are exempt from VAT if they are taking the goods out of the country within three months. The tax must be paid first, then claimed back. You must have your passport and return ticket with you; the shop assistant will help you complete the form VAT407—make sure you keep your part of it along with the export sales bill. Show Customs this form and have your goods ready to show.

BOND STREET

Bond Street mixes haute-couture outlets with art galleries. Asprey & Garrard, one of the world's great luxury stores, is here, as are the Fine Art Society and Sotheby's.
✚ F5 ✉ Mayfair, W1 🚇 Bond Street or Green Park

BROMPTON CROSS

Sophisticated fashion and design stores. The Conran Shop, selling quality design furniture, is the longest-established retailer.
✚ D7 ✉ Knightsbridge/Chelsea, SW3 🚇 Knightsbridge or South Kensington

JERMYN STREET

Once the local street for aristocrats swarming around St. James's Palace; the atmosphere of Jermyn Street remains select: Floris the perfumier (est. 1730); Paxton & Whitfield for cheeses; and Harvie & Hudson or Turnbull & Asser (➤ 78) for shirts.
✚ F6 ✉ St. James's, SW1 🚇 Piccadilly Circus or Green Park

KENSINGTON CHURCH STREET

This once-quiet lane now has more than 50 antique shops, Clarke's restaurant bakery and Kensington Place.
✚ B6 ✉ Kensington, W8 🚇 Notting Hill Gate or High Street Kensington

NEAL STREET

The epitome of Covent Garden's successful rebirth, this pedestrian street is packed with exotic little shops: Neal Street East, the Kite Store and, in Neal's Yard, a feast of wholefoods.
✚ G5 ✉ Covent Garden, WC2 🚇 Covent Garden

COVENT GARDEN PIAZZA

Most people make at least one visit to the Piazza where London's first square and subsequent fruit and vegetable market was pedestranized in the 1970s, accommodating dozens of small shops, crraft stalls and restaurants.
✚ G5 ✉ Covent Garden Piazza 🚇 Covent Garden

OXFORD STREET

The capital's main shopping artery and best-known shopping street. At the west end near Marble Arch is the largest branch of Marks & Spencer in the city; in the middle is the revamped Selfridges & Co and branches of all significant chains from Body Shop to Gap and John Lewis; at the east end are Tottenham Court Road's electrical and home stores.
✚ E5–G5 ✉ Mayfair/Marylebone, W1 🚇 Oxford Circus, Bond Street, Marble Arch, Tottenham Court Road

REGENT STREET

With its dramatic curve north from Piccadilly, John Nash's street is as smart as intended: Tower Records, Austin Reed, Burberry, Aquascutum, the sumptuous Café Royal, Mappin & Webb (silver), Hamleys (toys ➤ 60), Liberty (➤ 73) and the Disney store.
✚ F5 ✉ Mayfair/Soho, W1 🚇 Piccadilly Circus or Oxford Street

Department Stores

FORTNUM & MASON

Before going in, do not miss the clock, which has Messrs. Fortnum and Mason mincing forward each hour. Prices are high, but the shop-brand goods make perfect presents.
✚ F6 ✉ 181 Piccadilly, W1
☎ 020 7734 8040
🚇 Piccadilly Circus or Green Park

GENERAL TRADING COMPANY

Chic, small-scale department store with quality buys in all areas from china to gardening. Good mail-order catalogue.
✚ E7 ✉ 2 Symons Street, SW1 ☎ 020 7730 0411
🚇 Sloane Square

HARRODS

This vast emporium contains just about everything anyone could want. Apart from the revamped fashion departments, do not miss the spectacular food halls. Some 23 restaurants and bars provide refreshment.
✚ D6 ✉ 87–135 Brompton Road, SW1 ☎ 020 7730 1234
🚇 Knightsbridge

HARVEY NICHOLS

London's classiest clothes shop, from its original storefront window displays to the well-stocked fashion floors.
✚ E6 ✉ 67 Brompton Road, SW1 ☎ 020 7235 5000
🚇 Knightsbridge

JOHN LEWIS

Its slogan, 'never knowingly undersold', inspires a confidence that prices are solidly fair.
✚ F5 ✉ Oxford Street, W1
☎ 020 7629 7711 🚇 Oxford Circus

LIBERTY

Offering everything from sumptuous fabrics to china and glass, this shop's quality is characterized by exoticism and cutting-edge fashion mixed with an Arts and Crafts heritage and a beautiful mock-Tudor buiding.
✚ F5 ✉ 210–220 Regent Street, W1 ☎ 020 7734 1234
🚇 Oxford Circus

MARKS & SPENCER

Most people buy something at M&S. Clothes now have sharper styles, and the food departments offer an exceptional range of pre-prepared meals.
✚ E5 ✉ 458 Oxford Street, W1 ☎ 020 7935 7954
🚇 Marble Arch

PETER JONES

After a total renovation, this sister store to John Lewis, is back in the top league of London one-stop shopping experiences. Quality good design and sensible staff, plus advisory, packing and pampering services. Café and cocktail bar.
✚ E7 ✉ Sloane Square, SW1 ☎ 020 7730 3434 🚇 Sloane Square

SELFRIDGES

Less glitzy than Harrods, but equally good for the whole family. This vast, bedazzling store, which underwent a dramatic facelift in 2001, stocks beauty products, designer labels, china, glass and electrical goods. The food hall is worth exploring.
✚ E5 ✉ 400 Oxford Street, W1 ☎ 08708 377377
🚇 Marble Arch or Bond Street

ONE-STOP SHOPPING

The one-stop shopping that department stores offer has several advantages over slogging around the streets. If it rains, you stay dry. If you are hungry, there are cafés. There are also the services to be considered. Your purchases from various departments can be held for you while you shop, to be collected together at the end. Garments can be altered, presents wrapped and writing paper printed. And most stores have dependable after-sales service if something is not right.

Street Markets

SPECIALITY SHOPS

Speciality shops come in every shape and size. Stanley Gibbons (✉ 399 Strand, WC2 ☎ 020 7836 8444) is a philatelist's paradise, while James Smith & Sons (✉ 53 New Oxford Street, W1 ☎ 020 7836 4731) stocks every kind of umbrella to keep British rain at bay. Other favourites include the Crafts Council Shop (✉ 44 Pentonville Road, N1 ☎ 020 7806 2559, and at the V&A ▶ 30); Paperchase (✉ 213 Tottenham Court Road, W1 ☎ 020 7467 6200, plus many branches) and Smythson's (✉ 40 New Bond Street, W1 ☎ 020 7629 8558, and in Sloane Street), both stationers. BBC World Service Shop (✉ Bush House, Strand, WC2 ☎ 020 7557 2576; ✉ 50 Margaret Street, W1 ☎ 020 7631 4523) stock videos, cassettes and books related to their programmes; ideal for presents.

To find the speciality shop you want, use the Yellow Pages telephone directory, which is listed by subject.

SMITHFIELD MEAT MARKET

Smithfields (EC1) is the only large, fresh-food, commercial market left in central London. Thousands of bloody carcasses hung up on iron hooks are traded in Horace Jones's grand 19th-century building. Trading starts at 4am and the market closes down at noon (Mon–Fri).

ALFIE'S ANTIQUE MARKET

A huge space where the keen eyed seek out 20th-century decorative arts, antiques and vintage clothing. It's probably best to get an overview before focusing in on actually buying.

✚ D4 ✉ 134–25 Church Street, NW8 ☎ 020 7723 6066 🕓 Tue–Sat 10–6 🚇 Edgware Road or Marylebone

BERMONDSEY (NEW CALEDONIAN MARKET)

You need to know your stuff here—and, as the big dealers and auction-house experts get here before dawn, the earlier you go the better.

✚ L7 ✉ Long Lane and Bermondsey Street, SE1 🕓 Fri 5–2 🚇 Borough or London Bridge

BRIXTON MARKET

Best to go on Saturday, when the streets buzz with local African and Caribbean community shoppers buying their mangoes, sweet potatoes, snapper fish, calf's feet and ready-cooked delicacies.

✚ Off map at H10 ✉ Brixton Station Road, Electric Avenue and Popes Road, SW9 🕓 Mon, Tue, Thu–Sat 8.30–5.30; Wed 8.30–1 🚇 Brixton 🚉 Brixton

CAMDEN MARKETS

The small, vibrant market in Camden Lock has expanded and spawned other markets to fill every patch of space from the Underground station up to Hawley Road. Find crafts, clothes, books and more.

✚ E2 ✉ Camden High Street to Chalk Farm Road, NW1 🕓 Daily 10–6 with more stalls at weekends 🚇 Camden Town

CAMDEN PASSAGE

Bargain at the large, twice-weekly open-air antiques market held in front of the antiques stores; then try Chapel Street market across Upper Street.

✚ H3 ✉ Islington, N1 🕓 Wed 7–4, Sat 7–5 🚇 Angel

GREENWICH MARKET

Hundreds of stands selling antiques and crafts, clothes, old books and more. A good start to a Greenwich day (▶ 20).

✉ College Approach, Stockwell Street and corner of High Road and Royal Hill, SE10 🕓 Sat, Sun 9–6 🚉 Cutty Sark or Island Gardens DLR then walk through the tunnel

LEADENHALL MARKET

A surprising City treat housed under Horace Jones's 1880s arcades, with quality butchers, cheesemongers, fish-mongers and pubs.

✚ K5 ✉ Leadenhall, EC3 🕓 Mon–Fri 7–4 🚇 Bank or Monument

PORTOBELLO MARKET

Saturday is the big day, when antiques and not-so-antiques are sold from the shops and the solid line of vendors in front of them. There are lower prices further down the hill, with second-hand stands beneath Westway.

✚ B5 ✉ Portobello Road, W11 🕓 Fruit and vegetables/general Mon–Wed 9–5, Thu 9–1, Fri–Sat 7–6. Antiques Sat 7–5 🚇 Ladbroke Grove

Art & Antiques

AGNEWS

This internationally renowned art gallery has been going since 1817, Specializes in European Old Masters from the 13th to the mid-19th centuries; British art from the 17th to the 20th centuries; in particular the Victorian era.
➕ F6 ✉ 43 Old Bond Street, W1 ☎ 020 7629 4359
🚇 Green Park

ANTIQUARIUS

London's oldest antiques complex houses around 100 dealers whose goods include lace, old clothes and jewellery; there are plenty of quirky, affordable items here.
➕ D8 ✉ 131–41 King's Road, SW3 ☎ 020 7351 5353
🚇 Sloane Square

BONHAM'S

The strength of this auction house lies in its 20th-century and specialist sales. Less expensive goods are sold in its Chelsea Galleries.
➕ D7 ✉ Montpelier Galleries, Montpelier Street, SW7 ☎ 020 7393 3900 🚇 Knightsbridge

CHRISTIE'S

The auction house has departments ranging from grand old masters to coins and tribal art. A second, less expensive sale room is in South Kensington.
➕ F6 ✉ Christie's International Ltd., 8 King Street, SW1 ☎ 020 7839 9060 🚇 Green Park

THE FINE ART SOCIETY

One of the oldest and friendliest galleries in town.
➕ F5 ✉ 148 New Bond Street, W1 ☎ 020 7629 5116
🚇 Bond Street

GRAY'S ANTIQUE MARKET

High-quality goods ranging from pictures to silver are sold at around 170 stands.
➕ E5 ✉ 1–7 Davies Mews and 58 Davies Street, W1 ☎ 020 7629 7034
🚇 Bond Street

LOTS ROAD CHELSEA AUCTION GALLERIES

Eclectic mix of antique, reproduction and good contemporary designer furniture.
➕ C9 ✉ 71–4 Lots Road, SW10 ☎ 020 7351 7771
🚇 Sloane Square then it's a 20-minute walk or bus No. 19 or 22

SOTHEBY'S

The world's largest auction house. A rabbit warren of sale rooms with objects of all kinds on display. The 'Colonnade' sales are less expensive.
➕ F5 ✉ 34 New Bond Street, W1 ☎ 020 7293 5000
🚇 Bond Street

SPINK & SON

Best known for their coins, medals, stamps and banknotes.
➕ G4 ✉ 69 Southampton Row, WC1 ☎ 020 7563 4000
🚇 Holborn

WADDINGTON GALLERIES

In a small street lined with about 20 galleries selling modern art, Waddington is just one worth seeing; try also Theo Waddington, Redfern and Browse & Darby. Also worth exploring are Clifford and Derring Streets nearby.
➕ F5 ✉ 11 Cork Street, W1 ☎ 020 7851 2200 🚇 Green Park

BUYING AT AUCTION

Watching an auction is one thing; buying is quite another. At the pre-sale viewing, inspect any lot you may bid for and check its description and estimated sale price in the catalogue. If you cannot attend the sale, leave a bid; if you can, decide on your maximum bid and do not go above it! Bid by lifting your hand up high. If successful, pay and collect after the sale, or arrange for delivery.

PRIVATE GALLERIES

An indispensible tool for visitors getting to grips with commercial art galleries in London is the monthly *Galleries* magazine, available free from most galleries. With its maps and specialist subject index, information can be called up by area as well as subject.

MUSEUM & GALLERY SHOPS

You'll find an excellent source of material in these shops both for gifts and general interest. The following are some of the best:
British Museum (► 64) Books, games and design objects.
Design Museum (► 52) Chic designer goods.
National Gallery (► 41) Posters, diaries and books.
Natural History Museum (► 28) Dinosaurs galore; books, toys, games, plus serious natural history books.
Tate Britain (► 36) and **Tate Modern** (► 47) Books, prints, posters and gifts.
Victoria & Albert Museum (► 30) Books, unique crafts, toys and many collection-inspired goods.

75

Books, New & Old

BOOKSHOPS & CAFÉS

To browse in a bookshop with its own in-house café, try Borders Books, Music and Cafe (✉ 203 Oxford Street, W1 ☎ 020 7292 1600); their Charing Cross Road branch also has a café. Central London branches of Books Etc with cafés include those on Charing Cross Road, Oxford Street and Piccadilly. Waterstone's superstore (see this page) on Piccadilly has a café, juice bar and restaurant.

ELECTRONIC BARGAINS

To Europeans, London prices for electrical goods seem good value; to Americans they seem expensive. If you know what you want, compare prices up and down Tottenham Court Road for stereos, and look there as well as New Oxford Street for computers. Micro Anvika, on Tottenham Court Road, is good for hardware, software and CD-ROMs. If daunted, go to John Lewis, Selfridges or Harrods (➤ 73); all have good after sales service.

BERNARD QUARITCH

It is best to make an appointment to come to this, the most splendid and serious of the city's antiquarian bookshops.
➕ F5 ✉ 5 Lower John Street, W1 ☎ 020 7734 2983
Ⓜ Piccadilly Circus

BOOKS FOR COOKS

Possibly the world's best selection of books about cooking and cuisine; orders are taken and dispatched worldwide. Sample different recipes everyday.
➕ A5 ✉ 4 Blenheim Crescent, W11 ☎ 020 7221 1992
Ⓜ Ladbroke Grove

CINEMA BOOKSHOP

London's greatest selection of books on the film world ever. Well-informed staff, plus mail order.
➕ G5 ✉ 13–14 Great Russell Street, WC1 ☎ 020 7637 0206
Ⓜ Tottenham Court Road

DAUNT BOOKS

In his panelled and stained-glass elegant 1910 shop, James Daunt keeps an impressive stock of travelogues and guides.
➕ E4 ✉ 83–84 Marylebone High Street, W1 ☎ 020 7224 2295 Ⓜ Baker Street

FORBIDDEN PLANET

An amazing selection of fantasy, horror, science fiction; plus comic books.
➕ G5 ✉ 179 Shaftesbury Avenue, WC2 ☎ 020 7420 3666 Ⓜ Tottenham Court Road

HATCHARDS

Opened in 1797; past patrons have included British army commander, the Duke of Wellington (1769–1852) and four-time prime minister William Gladstone (1809–98). With their well-informed staff, Hatchards still knows how to make book buying a delicious experience.
➕ F6 ✉ 187 Piccadilly, W1 ☎ 020 7439 9921
Ⓜ Piccadilly Circus or Green Park

MAGGS BROTHERS

Make your appointment, then step into this Mayfair mansion to find an out-of-print book, a first edition or rare antiquarian book.
➕ E6 ✉ 50 Berkeley Square, W1 ☎ 020 7493 7160
Ⓜ Green Park

STANFORDS

London's largest selection of maps of countries, cities and even very small towns around the world, together with travel books.
➕ G5 ✉ 12–14 Long Acre, WC2 ☎ 020 7836 1321
Ⓜ Covent Garden

WATERSTONE'S

Europe's largest bookshop stocks more than 250,000 titles and has a restaurant, café and internet area.
➕ F6 ✉ 203–6 Piccadilly, W1 ☎ 020 7851 2400
Ⓜ Piccadilly Circus

ZWEMMER ARTS BOOKSHOP

Art books fill three neighbouring bookshops divided by category. Here, fine art is upstairs, decorative art and architecture downstairs. Photography and media at 80 Charing Cross Road; Graphic Design at 72 Charing Cross Road.
➕ G5 ✉ 24 Litchfield Street, WC2 ☎ 020 7240 4158
Ⓜ Leicester Square

China & Glass

ARAM DESIGNS LTD

Aram's international modern design. Stock includes furniture, lighting and glass.
➕ G5 ✉ 110 Drury Lane, WC2 ☎ 020 7557 7557 Ⓜ Covent Garden

ARIA

Aria stocks modern international state-of-the-art design, with plenty of Italian pieces on display. There is a second shop across the road devoted to bathroom accessories.
➕ H2 ✉ 133 Upper Street, N1 ☎ 020 7226 1021 Ⓜ Angel

CERAMICA BLUE

Huge collection of functional and decorative contemporary ceramic designs, made exclusively by potters world wide.
➕ A5 ✉ 10 Blenheim Crescent, W11 ☎ 020 7727 0288 Ⓜ Ladbroke Grove or Notting Hill Gate

DESIGNER'S GUILD

Tricia Guild's store is a wonderland of exquisite design. Contemporary china, glass and fabrics.
➕ D8 ✉ 277 King's Road, SW3 ☎ 020 7351 5775 Ⓜ Sloane Square then 15 minutes' walk or bus 19 or 22

HEAL'S

A frontrunner of the Arts and Crafts movement in the 1920s, Heal's specializes in timeless contemporary furniture.
➕ F4 ✉ 196 Tottenham Court Road, W1 ☎ 020 7636 1666 Ⓜ Goodge Street

INFINITY

Some of the best modern glassware in town, specializing in wine glasses, goblets, fruit bowls and vases; colours are jewel-like.
➕ G5 ✉ 8 Upper St. Martin's Lane, WC2 ☎ 020 7497 1011 Ⓜ Leicester Square

JEANETTE HAYHURST

One of the few places to find old glass, especially British pieces. Also stocks interesting studio glass.
➕ B6 ✉ 32a Kensington Church Street, W8 ☎ 020 7938 1539 Ⓜ High Street Kensington

PURVES & PURVES

Alessi, Starck and a host of contemporary designers. Lighting, furniture and homeware, in exuberant shades and shapes.
➕ F4 ✉ 220–4 Tottenham Court Road, W1 ☎ 020 7580 8223 Ⓜ Goodge Street

THOMAS GOODE LTD

Collectors of Meissen and Dresden need look no further than this splendid showroom. Famous English names include Wedgwood, Minton, Spode & Royal Worcester.
➕ E6 ✉ 19 South Audley Street, W1 ☎ 020 7499 2823 Ⓜ Green Park or Bond Street

WATERFORD WEDGWOOD

The largest selection of hand-made, full lead crystal Waterford glass—all made in Ireland—and Wedgwood china. Will phone the factory for special orders, help customers search for designs no longer made, and ship goods worldwide.
➕ F5 ✉ 173–4 Piccadilly, W1 ☎ 020 7629 2614 Ⓜ Piccadilly Circus

Do not worry about breaking your valuable purchases on the way home; they can be packed and sent there for you, fully insured.

SILVER

English silver is one of the best antique buys because it has been hallmarked since the mid-17th century, so you know precisely what you are buying. To get a good look, wander the London Silver Vaults on Chancery Lane , www.thesilvervaults.com, Antiquarius (► 75), Gray's Antique Market (► 75), Asprey's (✉ 169 New Bond Street, W1 ☎ 020 7493 6767), Mappin & Webb (✉ 170 Regent Street, W1 ☎ 020 7734 3801). Buy at these locations or visit Christine Schell (✉ 15 Cale Street, SW3 ☎ 020 7352 5563) for silver and tortoiseshell or John Jesse (✉ 160 Kensington Church Street, W8 ☎ 020 7229 0312) for art deco.

Fashion

FASHION

London is a byword for fashion innovation, as well as home to some of the best in traditional tailoring. To buy international high fashion, explore Harvey Nichols (▶ 73) and the shops lining Knightsbridge, Sloane Street, Brompton Cross, Beauchamp Place, Bond Street, South Molton Street and St. Christopher's Place. For more dramatic, innovative, streetwise fashion, Urban Outfitters (see this page), then visit Vivienne Westwood (✉ 44 Conduit Street, W1 ☎ 020 7439 1109), American Retro (✉ 35 Old Compton Street, W1 ☎ 020 7734 3477), Carhartt (✉ 56 Neal Street, WC2 ☎ 020 7836 5659), and Duffer of St. George (✉ 29 Shorts Gardens, WC2 ☎ 020 7379 4660). For high fashion men's wear, all close together in Sloane Avenue, try Paul Smith's flagship store (✉ 84 Sloane Avenue, SW3 ☎ 020 7589 9139), Joseph (✉ 74 Sloane Avenue, SW3 ☎ 020 7591 0808, many branches) and Kenzo (✉ 70 Sloane Avenue, SW3 ☎ 020 7225 1960).

ANDERSON & SHEPPARD

Thought by some to be the best tailor's shop on Savile Row, Anderson's was established in 1906. Hand-crafted suits by expert tailors result in very high prices.

➕ F5 ✉ 30 Savile Row, W1 ☎ 020 7734 1420 Ⓖ Piccadilly Circus or Oxford Circus

BRORA

Cashmere in an array of shades for men, women and children. Located on the King's Road among some other good shops, Brora is pricey but the quality is great.

➕ D8 ✉ 344 King's Road, SW3 ☎ 020 7352 3697 Ⓖ South Kensington

BROWNS

If it's up-to-the-minute labels you want come to this well-established shop near Bond Street station. For younger fashion try No.38 across the road and for sale items No. 49.

➕ E5 ✉ 23–27 South Molton Street, W1 ☎ 020 7514 0000 Ⓖ Bond Street

DESIGNER WAREHOUSE SALES

Behind King's Cross train station, bargains galore plus special annual Nicole Farhi nd Ghost sales.

➕ G3 ✉ 45 Balfe Street, N1 ☎ 020 7704 1064 Ⓖ King's Cross

JIMMY CHOO

Guaranteed to sell the highest-heeled shoes in town. Set in the affluent Brompton Cross area it's worth taking a look and try something on.

➕ D7 ✉ 169 Draycott Avenue, SW3 ☎ 020 7584 6111 Ⓖ South Kensington

KOH SAMUI

Many boutiques in London stock top British designers but Koh Samui has known names as well as the names of the future displaying a wealth of new talent in its Covent Garden shop.

➕ G5 ✉ 66–67 Monmouth Street, WC2 ☎ 020 7240 4280 Ⓖ Covent Garden or Leicester Square

LULU GUINNESS

Sleek modern shop selling quirky 1950's handbags, hats and shoes. Bags in every shape, from spiders' webs to flower baskets. Celebrities shop here. Also a branch in the City's Royal Exchange.

➕ E7 ✉ 3 Ellis Street, SW1 ☎ 020 7823 4828 Ⓖ Sloane Square

TURNBULL & ASSER

If you want tradition and classic British design, then this is the shop for men who follow royalty when buying a shirt. Made to measure or off the peg, pricey but superb quality and service.

➕ F6 ✉ 71–72 Jermyn Street, SW1 ☎ 020 7808 3000 Ⓖ Green Park or Piccadilly Circus

URBAN OUTFITTERS

Always changing; always supplying the trend-conscious young. Check out the latest and browse through the streetwear and newest accessories. Other branches.

➕ B6 ✉ 36–8 Kensington High Street, W8 ☎ 020 7761 1001 Ⓖ High Street Kensington

Food & Wine

BERRY BROS & RUDD

Opened as a grocer in 1699; the wines range from popular varieties to speciality madeiras, ports and clarets. Their own-label bottles are also good value. Perfect service.

🏠 F6 ✉ 3 St. James's Street, SW1 ☎ 020 7396 9600
Ⓜ Green Park

CARLUCCIO'S

This designer deli chain stocks only the most refined goods, such as truffle oil, black pasta and balsamic vinegar.

🏠 G5 ✉ 28A Neal Street, WC2 ☎ 020 7240 1487
Ⓜ Covent Garden

FRESH & WILD

Glorious organic foods, plus ready-to-eat and a juice bar. Five other London branches.

🏠 F2 ✉ 49 Parkway, NW1 ☎ 020 7428 7575 Ⓜ Camden Town

HAYNES HANSON & CLARK

This is a treat for the connoisseur, especially those keen on Burgundy. Much buying is direct from the wine estates.

🏠 E7 ✉ 25 Eccleston Street, SW1 ☎ 020 7259 0102
Ⓜ Knightsbridge

NEAL'S YARD DAIRY

A temple to the British cheese, where more than 50 varieties from small farms in Britain are ripened to perfection.

🏠 G5 ✉ 17 Shorts Gardens, WC2 ☎ 020 7240 5700
Ⓜ Covent Garden

ODDBINS

With more than 60 branches in London, Oddbins' wines are strong on quality, range and price.

🏠 G5 ✉ 23 Earlham Street, WC2 ☎ 020 7836 6331
Ⓜ Covent Garden

ROCOCO

Delicious, imaginative chocolates—go for artisan bars flavoured with Earl Grey tea, chilli pepper, nutmeg, cardamom or wild mint leaves.

🏠 D8 ✉ 321 King's Road, SW3 ☎ 020 7352 5857 Ⓜ Sloane Square

R. TWINING & CO

The little, atmospheric shop where the tea merchant set up his business in 1706 .

🏠 H5 ✉ 216 Strand, WC2 ☎ 020 7353 3511 Ⓜ Temple

TOM'S

Basement deli sells breads, patisserie, cheeses, cold meats, preserved lemons, olives and caviar. Bustling café on the first floor.

🏠 B5 ✉ 226 Westbourne Grove, W11 ☎ 020 7221 8818
Ⓜ Bayswater

VILLANDRY

Quality 'foodstore' with best buys taking in French and English cheeses, great breads, olive oil and much more.

🏠 F5 ✉ 170 Great Portland Street, W1N ☎ 020 7631 3131
Ⓜ Great Portland Street

VINOPOLIS

Mouthwatering breads, cheese, olives and of course, wines in a shop adjoining the wine tour (► 62).

🏠 J6 ✉ Bank End, SE1 ☎ 0870 241 4040
Ⓜ London Bridge

WINE

London has an unrivalled variety of international wines at the best prices, for, although Britain is not a major wine-producing country, the British like to drink wine and know about it. This explains the range, quality and fiercely competitive prices in the chains (Oddbins, Threshers) and the supermarkets (Sainsbury's, Safeway, Waitrose and Tesco). For bulk buying, consider the Majestic Warehouse chain, a reliable wine merchant, or Christie's and Sotheby's regular wine auctions (► 75).

MAKE A PICNIC

With so many parks and benches to choose from in London, a picnic makes a good break from a hard morning's sightseeing or shopping. The big stores have some of the most seductive food halls—and they stock wine; see Harrods, Selfridges, Fortnum & Mason and Marks & Spencer (all ► 73). Old Compton Street (► 72) is a food shopper's delight; see also Clarke's Bakery (✉ 122 Kensington Church Street, W8) and other cafés that sell their own prepared food to take out.

Theatre

THEATRE TIPS

If you care about where you sit, go in person and peruse the plan. For an evening 'Sold out' performance, it is worth waiting in line for returns; otherwise, try for a matinée. The most inexpensive seats could be far from the stage or uncomfortable, so take binoculars and a cushion. As for dress, Londoners rarely dress up for the theatre anymore; but they do order their interval drinks before the play starts, and remain seated while they applaud.

TICKET–BUYING TIPS

Use the tkts Half-price Ticket Booth (see this page). Preview tickets are lower in price, as are matinée tickets. Get up early and line up for one-day bargain tickets at the RNT and RSC. Go with friends and make a party booking at a reduced rate. Ask the National Theatre, Royal Court and other theatres about special discounts on particular performances; and keep student and senior citizen cards ready. Remember, the show is the same wherever you sit!

INFORMATION

Theatre in London covers a wide range of venues. It is vibrant, varied and extensive. *Time Out*, London's weekly entertainment guide, provides an exhaustive list of all theatres, plus reviews. Daily newspapers carry a less complete but totally up-to-date listing, with more reviews. Ticket prices are lowest for fringe, more expensive for West End, and very expensive for musicals.

TICKET BUYING

Telephone booking can be done using a credit card, which must be produced when collecting the tickets. If you reserve without a credit card, you must usually arrive at the theatre 40 minutes before curtain-up—or else the tickets will be put back for sale. Reserving in person means you can see the seating plan—a good idea if you want a decent seat in some of London's older theatres. Ask for information on leg room and sight lines.

TICKET AGENCIES

Ticketmaster ☎ 020 7344 4444 and First Call ☎ 020 7420 0000 are both reliable. You can call Globaltickets ☎ 0870 842 2248, a division of the huge Keith Prowse ticket agency. Some shows have no booking fee, others a small one, and a few rise to 22 per cent of the ticket price, so ask first. Beware: it is unwise to buy from small agencies, and extremely unwise to buy from ticket touts.

TKTS

Each day a limited number of tickets for some West End shows is sold for that day's performance at half price, plus a £2 service charge. The rules are: a maximum of two tickets per person and no exchanges or returns.
✚ G5 ⊠ Leicester Square, WC2 🕐 Mon–Sat 10–7, Sun noon–3 🚇 Leicester Square or Piccadilly Circus

THE THEATRE YEAR

At any one time there will be an average of 45 West End theatres playing a range of musicals, drama, comedy and thrillers, as well as staging opera and dance. LIFT (London International Festival of Theatre) spreads its festival night around the year, staging exciting productions in unusual venues. The Royal Shakespeare Company (RSC) holds an annual festival, often at the Almeida or Young Vic theatres.

WEST END THEATRES

The Society of London Theatre (SOLT) ☎ 020 7557 6700; www.official londontheatre.co.uk represents the owners, managers and producers of major London theatres and the rest of the UK. SOLT runs the annual Laurence Olivier Awards—London's answer to the Tonys—publishes the fortnightly London Theatre Guide (free from theaters) and runs a Theatre Token scheme ☎ 0870 164 8800 and the tkts Half-price Ticket Booth (see above).

ROYAL NATIONAL THEATRE (RNT)

British and world drama, classics and new plays. Home of the National Theatre company, it has three performance spaces—the Olivier, the Lyttelton and the Cottesloe. All have several productions in repertory. ⊞ H6 ✉ South Bank, SE1 ☎ Information and tours 020 7452 3400. Theatre tickets 020 7452 3000 ⊜ Embankment or Waterloo ⊜ Waterloo

ROYAL SHAKESPEARE THEATRE (RSC)

With no regular London home, go to www.rsc.org.uk to find out which RSC production is visiting which theatre.

THE YOUNG VIC

This serial award-winning dynamic theatre is performing around town while its Waterloo home is being rebuilt, to reopen in 2006. Visit the website www.youngvic.org for information on where to see its productions.

MUSICALS

The successful, long-running shows are dominated by the great impresarios. Sir Andrew Lloyd Webber, who restored and owns the Palace Theatre, has staged *Starlight Express*, *Sunset Boulevard*, *Phantom of the Opera* and *Cats*, the latter two with Cameron Mackintosh, and their *Les Misérables* adaptation of Victor Hugo's novel of the French Revolution, still continues to draw the crowds at the Palace.

LONG-RUNNING STALWARTS

Few plays have the sustained, long-running success of the musicals. Most famous is Agatha Christie's *The Mousetrap* at St. Martin's, having reached its 50th anniversary in 2002. At the Fortune Theatre, *The Woman in Black* began its run in 1989.

OFF–WEST END THEATRE

This new category honours the fringe theatres that stage major imaginative productions. Look in the listings for the Almeida, the Bush, Donmar Warehouse, Drill Hall, the Gate, Hampstead, King's Head, Lyric Studio, Riverside Studios, Royal Court, Theatre Royal Stratford East, Tricycle and the Young Vic.

FRINGE AND PUB THEATER

True fringe, or 'alternative' theatre in London is vibrant, varied and dotted about in over 35 venues, many of them pubs. Try Etcetera Theatre (at the Oxford Arms pub), Finborough, the Hen & Chickens, New End Theatre, Old Red Lion and the White Bear.

COMEDY

The Comedy Store is hugely popular. Also try the Banana Cabaret, Jongleurs chain of clubs, Comedy Café and Red Rose Comedy Club. There are also numerous venues for fringe comedy.

OPEN-AIR THEATRE

If the weather is good, grab a picnic and head for the Open Air Theatre, Regent's Park, box office: ☎ 020 7486 2431 (Jun–Sep) or Holland Park, box office: ☎ 0845 230 9769 (Jun–Aug).

CHILDREN'S THEATRE

Several theatres stage magical performances all year around. Names to look for include the Little Angel Theatre (☎ 020 7226 1787), a doyen of puppet theatres, Polka Children's Theatre (☎ 020 8543 4888) and the Unicorn Theatre for Children (☎ 020 7609 8753). Ask about children's productions at the National and the RSC, as well as Punch and Judy shows in Covent Garden Piazza.

REVIVED THEATRES

Some old London theatres have been revived. Andrew Lloyd Webber restored his 1880s Cambridge Theatre. The Theatre Royal, Haymarket, has new gold leaf, while the Savoy and the Criterion have been meticulously restored. Out of the West End, the Richmond Theatre is a treat. On the south bank, there is the splendidly ornate Old Vic Theatre and the small-scale Globe theatre opened in 1997, designed in the manner of Burbage's original where Shakespeare worked.

Classical Music, Opera & Ballet

MUSIC EVERYWHERE!

London is full of music. At lunchtime, the best places are churches, where the regular concerts are usually free. Look in *Time Out* listings (➤ 80) for: St. Anne and St. Agnes, and St. Olave's in the City; St. James's, Piccadilly; and St. Martin-in-the-Fields in Trafalgar Square. St. Paul's Cathedral has choral evensong at 5pm Mondays to Saturdays, 3.15 on Sundays. Generally Sundays in cathedrals and churches are best for sacred music. Look for concerts in historic houses, museums and galleries, especially during the City of London Festival (July). Finally, music is played outdoors in the royal parks, Embankment Gardens and elsewhere, but best of all at Kenwood (➤ 31) or Marble Hill, Richmond, on summer evenings.

THE MUSIC YEAR

Runs non stop. Look for festivals such as the City of London, Spitalfields, Almeida and Hampton Court Palace, and traditions such as the Christmas Oratorios, carol singing in Trafalgar Square and the Easter Passions. The major classic festival is the Proms, a nickname for the Henry Wood Promenade Concerts, held daily at the Royal Albert Hall and elsewhere from mid-July to mid-September, and broadcast live on BBC Radio 3.

THE DANCE YEAR

Highpoints include the Coliseum's summer season, the Royal Ballet's performances at the Royal Opera House and the Nutcracker Suite season at the Royal Festival Hall (Dec–Jan). Other major venues are: Barbican Centre, Sadler's Wells, the Place, ICA, Peacock Theatre and Riverside Studios. The climax of the year is Dance Umbrella, a world showcase for contemporary dance (Oct–Nov).

THE OPERA YEAR

Grand opera alternates with dance at the Royal Opera House. Cheaper and often more vibrant opera takes place at the larger Coliseum (performances in English). In addition, there are visits from Welsh National Opera, Opera North and Opera Factory, and open-air opera performances in Holland Park and by Kenwood Lake.

MAJOR VENUES

BARBICAN CONCERT HALL

✠ J4 ✉ Barbican Centre, Silk Street, EC2 ☎ 020 7638 8891, Mon–Sat 10–8, Sun noon–8, www.barbican.org.uk. Range of good ticket deals Ⓤ Barbican

LONDON COLISEUM

✠ G5 ✉ St. Martin's Lane, WC2 ☎ 020 7632 8300 Ⓤ Leicester Square

ROYAL ALBERT HALL

✠ C6 ✉ Kensington Gore, SW7 ☎ 020 7589 3203. Reservations 020 7589 8212 Ⓤ South Kensington

ROYAL OPERA HOUSE

Finally reopened in December 1999 after major refurbishment, this is the venue for opera and the home of the Royal Ballet.
✠ G5 ✉ Bow Street, Covent Garden, WC2 ☎ 020 7304 4000 Ⓤ Covent Garden

SADLER'S WELLS THEATRE

The most electrifying dance theatre in Europe, newly built for 2000—a must for all ballet fans.
✠ H3 ✉ Rosebery Avenue, EC1 ☎ 020 7863 8000 Ⓤ Angel

SOUTH BANK

Royal Festival Hall, Queen Elizabeth Hall and Purcell Room.
✠ G6–H6 ✉ South Bank, SE1 ☎ 020 7960 4242 Ⓤ Waterloo

WIGMORE HALL

Great classic concerts.
✠ E5 ✉ 36 Wigmore Street, W1 ☎ 020 7935 2141 Ⓤ Bond Street

Jazz & Pub Music

BARFLY

A Camden club that hosts more than 20 indie groups a week—some bad, some OK and some destined for stardom.

E1 ✉ 49 Chalk Farm Road, NW1 ☎ 020 7691 4244 Ⓜ Chalk Farm

BOSTON ARMS

A great variety of music, so phone before you set off for this fashionable pub in North London's Tufnell Park.

Off map at F1 ✉ 178 Junction Road, N19 ☎ 020 7272 81533 Ⓜ Tufnell Park

BULL'S HEAD, BARNES

Seductive combination of good jazz in the friendly village atmosphere of a riverside pub.

Off map at A10 ✉ 373 Lonsdale Road, SW13 ☎ 020 8876 5241 Ⓜ Barnes Bridge

DOVER STREET

Large, candle-lit, popular basement where the music can be jump jive, jazz, rhythm and blues or Big Band. The food is good.

F6 ✉ 8–9 Dover Street, W1 ☎ 020 7629 9813 Ⓜ Piccadilly Circus

JAZZ CAFÉ

Current favourite among the young; buzzes nightly with the widest range of jazz, from soul to rap.

F2 ✉ 5 Parkway, NW1 ☎ 020 7916 6060 Ⓜ Camden Town

MONARCH

Come and hear the Barfly's Club indie music in this Camden pub.

E2 ✉ 49 Chalk Farm Road, NW1 ☎ 020 7691 4244 Ⓜ Chalk Farm

PIZZA EXPRESS JAZZ CLUB

Quality pizzas and great, often mainstream, jazz in this friendly Soho cellar. Other branches of Pizza Express have live jazz, too.

F5 ✉ 10 Dean Street, W1 ☎ 020 7439 8722 Ⓜ Tottenham Court Road

PIZZA ON THE PARK

More upscale than its sister, Pizza Express; top foreign names play at one or other venue.

E6 ✉ 11 Knightsbridge, SW1 ☎ 020 7235 5273 Ⓜ Hyde Park Corner

RONNIE SCOTT'S

One of the world's best-known and most loved jazz clubs, run by jazz musicians for jazz lovers.

F5 ✉ 47 Frith Street, W1 ☎ 020 7439 0747 Ⓜ Tottenham Court Road

SMOLLENSKY'S ON THE STRAND

Live and varied jazz every Sunday night at this central bar-cum-restaurant in central location.

G5 ✉ 105 The Strand, WC2 ☎ 020 7497 2101 Ⓜ Charing Cross

VORTEX

A bit further out but this laidback café/restaurant is worth it for its live jazz.

Off map at K1 ✉ 139–141 Stoke Newington Church Street, N16 ☎ 020 7254 6516 Ⓜ Stoke Newington

606 CLUB

Find local and young jazz musicians in the Chelsea border haunt.

C9 ✉ 90 Lots Road, SW10 ☎ 020 7352 5953 Ⓜ Fulham Broadway

ALL THAT JAZZ

London boasts a great concentration of world-class jazz musicians, both homegrown and foreign, traditional and contemporary Evening and late-night gigs cover rock, roots, rhythm and blues and more, many in pubs. For a list of venues, check *Time Out*. Also check out the latest information on jazz on www.jazznights.co.uk

PUB MUSIC

This can be one of the least expensive and most enjoyable evenings out in London, worth the trip to an off-beat location. For the price of a pint of beer (usually a huge choice) you can settle down to enjoy the ambience and listen to some of the best alternative music available in town—from folk, jazz and blues to rhythm and blues, soul and more. Audiences tend to be friendly, loyal to their venue and happy to talk music.

Cinemas & Clubs

London lacks the range of cinemas to be found in some other capital cities and often receives foreign films long after their home release. But there is plenty of independent and late-night cinema, making a good beginning to a night of clubbing. Some cinema seats are half price on Mondays.

One-night clubbing is strong. To find the right club night and club style, consult *Time Out's* night-by-night listing (➤ 80) or see the advertisements at regular venues. Dress streetwise and pay at the door.

COCKTAILS AND BARS

For lively club-bars try Lab (✉ 12 Old Compton Street, W1 ☎ 020 7437 7820), Salt (✉ 82 Seymour Street, W2 ☎ 020 7402 1155), Sosho (✉ 2 Tabernacle Street, Shoreditch, EC2 ☎ 020 7920 0701), Alphabet Bar (✉ 61–63 Beak Street, W1 ☎ 020 7439 2190). For pampering cocktails, head for the Berkeley Hotel (➤ 86) Claridge's lounge (➤ 86). For New York style try the Dorchester (➤ 86); this and the Meridien Waldorf's atmospheric bar (✉ Aldwych, WC2 ☎ 0870 400 8484) is ideal pre- or post-theatre. To be seen, go to St, Martin's Lane Hotel (➤ 86). To be discreet, go to the Connaught (✉ 16 Carlos Place, W1 ☎ 020 7499 7070).

CINEMAS

THE BIG SCREENS

The places to see premiers and commercial first runs. Some of the biggest are the Empire (Cinema 1) and Odeon on Leicester Square, and the UGC Trocadero on Shaftesbury Avenue.

IMAX CINEMAS (➤ 60)

For a truly spectacular wraparound cinematic experience.

THE INDEPENDENTS

These cinemas show mainstream blockbusters, foreign (subtitled) and off-beat British films. The most sumptuous are Curzon Mayfair, Barbican and the Chelsea Cinema; others include the Screen chain, Gate, Renoir and Tricycle.

NATIONAL FILM THEATRE

Advantages of its three screens: good programming, silent audiences, film-specialist bookshop, riverside restaurant, children's screenings.
🚇 H6 ✉ South Bank, SE1 ☎ 020 7928 3232 🚇 Waterloo

REPERTORY

Good for old films, seasons, double-bills and late nights. Try the Everyman Riverside Studios; knife-edge contemporary at ICA Cinemathèque; variety at the Ciné Lumière in the French. Also go to the Museum of London's 'Made in London' series (➤ 49).

CLUB VENUES

The club scene is so liquid that many exciting clubs sometimes open and close within months. As well as checking the music, remember to check the dress code, the crowd (mixed/gay/lesbian), the entrance fee (fashionable venues are expensive) and also consider how much a late night taxi fare back home will cost.

THE END

Varied music in a well-designed West End club.
🚇 G5 ✉ 18A West Central Street, WC1 ☎ 020 7419 9199 🚇 Holborn or Tottenham Court Road

FABRIC

Dance and hang out with up to 2,500 others at this Clerkenwell super-club.
🚇 H4 ✉ 77A Charterhouse Street, EC1 ☎ 020 7336 8898 🚇 Leicester Square

MINISTRY OF SOUND

Glamorous and justly popular, this prison-like building is London's best-known club.
🚇 J7 ✉ 103 Gaunt Street, SE1 ☎ 020 7378 6528 🚇 Elephant & Castle

OCEAN

Hackney's super-tech music venue.
🚇 M2 ✉ 270 Mare Street, E8 ☎ 020 8533 0111 🚇 Hackney Central

SCALA

Hip hop, breakbeat and indie in this super-club. Three floors with viewing platforms.
🚇 G3 ✉ King's Cross, N1 ☎ 020 7833 2022 🚇 King's Cross

Spectator Sport

THE MAJOR VENUES

ALL ENGLAND LAWN TENNIS CHAMPIONSHIPS, WIMBLEDON

Tennis's top tournament starts late June. Enter the ticket ballot or line up for tickets, except on the last four days.

✉ All England Lawn Tennis and Croquet Club, Church Road, SW19 ☎ 020 8946 2244 🚇 Southfields

CRYSTAL PALACE NATIONAL SPORTS CENTRE

The major venue for national competitions.

✉ Ledrington Road, SE19 ☎ 020 8778 0131 🚆 Crystal Palace

LONDON ARENA

Only 15 minutes from central London, this sporting and entertainment venue is host to the Superleague London Knights ice hockey team.

✉ Limeharbour, Isle of Dogs, E14 ☎ 020 7538 1212 🚇 Docklands Light Railway (DLR) Crossharbour & London Arena

LORD'S CRICKET GROUND

Home of the MCC (Marylebone Cricket Club ➤ 62); watch Middlesex play home games, test cricket, major finals and Sunday league games.

✚ D3 ✉ St. John's Wood Road, NW8 ☎ 020 7432 1066 🚇 St. John's Wood

THE AMP OVAL

Surrey home games and test cricket; also Sunday league games.

✚ H8 ✉ Surrey County Cricket Club, The Oval, SE11 ☎ 020 7582 6660 🚇 Oval

ROYAL ALBERT HALL

Grand Victorian building holding 5,000 spectators; boxing, tennis and sumo-wrestling events.

✚ C6 ✉ Kensington Gore, SW7 ☎ 020 7589 8212 🚇 South Kensington

TWICKENHAM

Tickets for the internationals at Twickenham are scarce; it is easier to watch the Varsity match (Dec), the Cup Final (Apr–May) or take in a tour game.

OTHER MAJOR SPORTS

ASSOCIATION FOOTBALL (SOCCER)

Visit one of the top London clubs (Aug–May) such as Arsenal, Chelsea, Fulham or Tottenham Hotspur.

HORSE RACING

A British obsession, so there are plenty of races near London during the flat season (Mar–Nov) and winter steeple-chasing (Aug–May). On and off course, betting is legal and well governed. Daytime races at Epsom, Kempton Park and Ascot can be reached by train from London, or take the train out to Windsor or Kempton for a delightful summer evening meeting. Further out are Goodwood in West Sussex and Newmarket in Suffolk. Daily newspapers have details of race meetings.

You can watch and play most sports either in or near London (often merely an Underground ride away). Major events are held on Saturdays and Sundays; tickets are readily available (see ticket agencies ➤ 80).

PARTICIPATORY SPORTS

London's many parks and open spaces are alive with people playing tennis, bowls, cricket and football or jogging, walking and boating. For more formal sports, Crystal Palace National Sports Centre (see this page) has comprehensive facilities; but Kensington Leisure Centre (✉ Walmer Road, W1 ☎ 020 7727 9747), the Oasis (✉ 32 Endell Street, WC2 ☎ 020 7831 1804) and the Queen Mother Sports Centre (✉ 223 Vauxhall Bridge Road, SW1 ☎ 020 7630 5522) are more central. Barbican Health & Fitness Centre and Broadgate Club have good fitness equipment.

Luxury Hotels

PRICES

Expect to pay the following prices per night for a single room, excluding VAT:

Luxury   more than £280
Mid-range   £100–£280
Budget   less than £100

BARGAIN DEALS

To be pampered amid sumptuous surroundings may be an essential part of your holiday. London's most luxurious hotels have been built with no expense spared. Although London hotel prices are generally very high, quality rooms can be had for bargain prices. It's always worth asking when you make your reservation whether any special deals are available. Most deluxe and mid-range hotels offer weekend deals throughout the year, often including breakfast, dinner and sometimes theatre tickets. The big chains such as Forte, Mount Charlotte Thistle and Best Western have brochures offering package deals. Newly refurbished hotels usually have incentive prices, and off-season months such as January and February are a buyer's market.

BERKELEY

Ongoing refurbishment ensures that the 214 bedrooms are furnished with attention to detail. Health spa, rooftop pool and two restaurants.

✚ J2 ✉ Wilton Square, SW1 ☎ 020 7235 6000, fax 020 7235 4430, www.savoygroup.co.uk Ⓤ Hyde Park Corner

CLARIDGE'S

From the art-deco lobby and mirrored dining room to the huge baths and log fires in the corner suites, this is deluxe Mayfair living. 203 rooms.

✚ E5 ✉ Brook Street, W1 ☎ 020 7629 8860, fax 020 7499 2210, www.claridges.co.uk Ⓤ Bond Street

DORCHESTER

Deliciously art deco, a London landmark from its grand entrance and piano bar to its Oliver Messel suite. 250 rooms.

✚ E6 ✉ Park Lane, W1 ☎ 020 7629 8888, fax 020 7409 0114, www.dorchesterhotel.com Ⓤ Green Park, Hyde Park Corner

HALKIN HOTEL

Central London's first deluxe hotel built and furnished in contemporary design throughout, with a suitably upscale Thai restaurant. 41 rooms.

✚ E6 ✉ 4 Halkin Street, SW1 ☎ 020 7333 1000, fax 020 7333 1100, www.halkin.co.uk Ⓤ Hyde Park Corner

MANDARIN ORIENTAL HYDE PARK

New owners are injecting new life back into this grand hotel. With top-class service, you also get stunning views over Hyde Park. 200 rooms.

✚ E6 ✉ 66 Knightsbridge, SW1 ☎ 020 7235 2000, fax 020 7235 4552, www.mandarinoriental.com Ⓤ Knightsbridge

METROPOLITAN

Lush Hyde Park views with contrasting minimal interiors. 155 rooms.

✚ E6 ✉ Old Park Lane, W1 ☎ 020 7447 10000, fax 020 7447 1100, www.metropolitan.co.uk Ⓤ Hyde Park Corner

ONE ALDWYCH

This stylish contemporary hotel in an Edwardian building epitomizes London's current hotel fashion restrained luxury. 105 rooms.

✚ G5 ✉ 1 Aldwych, WC2 ☎ 020 7300 1000, fax 020 7300 1001, www.onealdwych.com Ⓤ Covent Garden or Temple

THE RITZ

Small but sumptuous, with plenty of old style, gilt decor and the great first-floor promenade to London's most beautiful dining room, overlooking Green Park. 133 rooms.

✚ F6 ✉ 150 Piccadilly, W1 ☎ 020 7493 8181, fax 020 7493 2687, www.ritzlondon.com Ⓤ Green Park

ST. MARTIN'S LANE

Theatrical minimalism at Ian Schrager and Philippe Starck's fabulously located hotel that opened in 1999; art, theatre, opera and restaurants are a mere step away. 204 rooms.

✚ G5 ✉ St. Martin's Lane, WC2 ☎ 020 7300 5500, fax 020 7300 5501, www.ianschrangerhotels.com Ⓤ Covent Garden or Leicester Square

Mid-Range Hotels

ACADEMY

Excellent location for the British Museum. Set in five converted Georgian town houses with exceptionally light, modern rooms. 50 rooms.
➕ F4 ✉ 21 Gower Street, WC1 ☎ 020 7631 4115, fax 020 7636 3442, www.etontownhouse.com 🚇 Goodge Street

BLAKES

Sumptuous decadence achieved by designer Anoushka Hempel. 51 rooms.
➕ C8 ✉ 33 Roland Gardens, SW7 ☎ 020 7370 6701, fax 020 7373 0442, www. blakes hotels.com 🚇 South Kensington

CHARLOTTE STREET HOTEL

Kit and Tim Kemp's boutique cocktail of serious comfort and fairytale Englishness with 52 rooms.
➕ F4 ✉ 15 Charlotte Street, W1 ☎ 020 7806 2000, fax 020 7806 2002 🚇 Goodge Street

COVENT GARDEN HOTEL

Another of Kit and Tim Kemp's stylish boutique hotels, this one attracts film stars who enjoy its 58 traditional yet contemporary British rooms, bathrooms and library.
➕ F5 ✉ 10 Monmouth Street, WC2 ☎ 020 7806 1000, fax 020 7806 1100, www.firm dalehotels.com 🚇 Leicester Square

GORING

High standards of old-fashioned hospitality and service make this splendid hotel memorable. Owned by the Goring family for almost a century. 74 rooms. Stylish reception rooms for afternoon tea and cocktails.
➕ F7 ✉ Beeston Place, Grosvenor Gardens, SW1 ☎ 020 7396 9000, fax 020 7834 4393, www.goringhotel.com 🚇 Victoria

THE LEONARD

Discreet, stylish small hotel, near Oxford Street; comfortable, superbly decorated bedrooms. 28 rooms.
➕ D5 ✉ 15 Seymour Street, W1 ☎ 020 7935 2010, fax 020 7935 6700, www.theleonard. com 🚇 Marble Arch

PORTOBELLO

Romantic retreat with exotic, sumptuous rooms, close to the antiques shops of Portobello Road. 24 rooms.
➕ A5 ✉ 22 Stanley Gardens, W11 ☎ 020 7727 2777, fax 020 7792 9641 🚇 Notting Hill Gate

ROOKERY

Discreet comforts in this wonderfully atmospheric small hotel in Clerkenwell, with antiques, open fires and Victorian bathrooms. 33 rooms.
➕ H4 ✉ 12 St. Peter's Lane, EC1 ☎ 020 7336 0931, fax 020 7336 0932, www. hazlittshotel.com 🚇 Farringdon

THE TRAFALGAR

Hard to beat this boutique hotel for its central location, congenial buzzy atmosphere, classy cocktails and smart but simple rooms. 129 rooms.
➕ G6 ✉ 2 Spring Gardens, SW1 ☎ 020 7970 2900, fax 020 7870 2911, www.hilton. co.uk 🚇 Charing Cross

BEWARE OF HIDDEN HOTEL COSTS

The room price quoted by a hotel may, or may not, include continental breakfast or full English breakfast and VAT, which is currently 17½ per cent. Since these affect the final bill dramatically, it is vital to ask in advance. Also, check the percentage mark-up on telephone calls, which can be high–there may even be charges for using a telephone charge card or receiving a fax; and ask about the laundry and pressing service, which can be very slow.

MODERN HOTELS

London has a plethora of contemporary hotels, from starkly minimal to sumptuously luxurious. At the top end, try the Metropolitan, One Aldwych, St. Martins's Lane (▶ 86) and the Hempel (✉ 31–35 Craven Hill, W2 ☎ 020 7298 9000, www.the-hempel.co.uk). In the mid-range try Schrager's Sanderson (✉ 50 Berners Street, W1 ☎ 020 7300 1400, www.ianschragerhotels.com), No. 5 Maddox Street (✉ 5 Maddox Street, W1 ☎ 020 7647 0200), myhotel Bloomsbury (✉ 11–13 Bayley Street, Bedford Square, W1 ☎ 020 7667 6000, www.myhotels.co.uk; there is a second myhotel in Chelsea) and the renovated Great Eastern Hotel (✉ Liverpool Street, EC2 ☎ 020 7618 5000, www.great-eastern-hotel.co.uk).

Budget Accommodation

LOCATION IS EVERYTHING

It is well worth perusing the London map to decide where you are likely to spend most of your time. Then select a hotel in that area or accessible to it by Underground on a direct line, so you avoid having to change trains. London is vast and it takes time to cross it, particularly by bus and costly taxis. By paying a little more to be in the heart of the city and near your activities, you will save on travel time and costs.

BED & BREAKFAST

Stay in a carefully chosen private house in London for both the venue and the friendliness of the hosts. Prices to suit all budgets.

London Bed and Breakfast Agency
✉ 71 Fellows Road, NW3 3JY
☎ 020 7586 2768, fax 020 7586 6567,
www.londonbb.com

YOUTH HOSTELS

There are seven hostels in central London (by Oxford Street, in Holland Park and by St. Paul's Cathedral, for example), so reserve well ahead.

Youth Hostels Association
✉ Trevelyan House, Dimple Road, Matlock, Derbyshire, DE4 3YH ☎ 0870 770 8868, (+44 1629 592700 from outside UK); reservations 0870 770 6113 (+44 1629 592708 from outside UK);
www.yha.org.uk

EURO HOTEL

Stylish Bloomsbury setting for a small, charming bed and breakfast. 35 rooms.
✚ G4 ✉ 51–3 Cartwright Gardens, Russell Square, WC1 ☎ 020 7387 4321, fax 020 7383 5044, www.eurohotel.co.uk Ⓜ Russell Square

GENERATOR

This stylish, industrial-style building offers 800 guests bunk-bedded rooms but excellent facilities. 217 rooms.
✚ G4 ✉ Compton Place, Tavistock Place, WC1 ☎ 020 7388 7666, fax 020 7388 7644, www.the-generator.co.uk Ⓜ Russell Square

INTERNATIONAL STUDENTS HOUSE

Rooms and family flats by Regent's Park. Reserve well ahead. 304 rooms.
✚ F4 ✉ 229 Great Portland Street, W1 ☎ 020 7631 8300, fax 020 7631 8315 Ⓜ Great Portland Street or Regent's Park

KENSINGTON MANOR

Well-placed for South Kensington museums and Knightsbridge shopping. 14 rooms.
✚ C7 ✉ 8 Emperors Gate, SW7 ☎ 020 7370 7516, fax 020 7373 3163 Ⓜ Gloucester Road

LONDON HOMESTEAD SERVICES

Try this agency if you want to stay with a London family: over 200 homes within 20 minutes of Piccadilly. Minimum three-night stay.
✉ 3 Coombe Wood Road, Kingston-upon-Thames, Surrey ☎ 020 8949 4455, fax 020 8549 5492

SWISS HOUSE HOTEL

Comfortable little hotel in a pretty area of South Kensington. 15 rooms.
✚ C8 ✉ 171 Old Brompton Road, SW5 ☎ 020 7373 2769, fax 020 7373 4983, www.swisshousehotel.com Ⓜ Earl's Court or Gloucester Road

TRAVEL INN CAPITAL

Practical, no frills chain whose star London location is in County Hall, opposite the Houses of Parliament. 313 rooms.
✚ G6 ✉ County Hall, Belvedere Road, SE1 ☎ 0870 238 3300, fax 020 7902 1619, www.travelinn.co.uk Ⓜ Waterloo

TRAVELODGE

Located in a quiet spot not far from Liverpool Street Station, this hotel provides 142 adequate rooms at good rates. Ideal for families.
✚ K5 ✉ 1 Harrow Lodge, E1 ☎ 0870 191 1689, www.travelodge.co.uk Ⓜ Liverpool Street

UNIVERSITY WOMEN'S CLUB

Located in an old Mayfair house; membership open to all women graduates and similarly qualified women; friends pay a temporary membership fee. 24 rooms.
✚ E6 ✉ 2 Audley Square, South Audley Street, W1 ☎ 020 7499 2268, fax 020 7499 7046 Ⓜ Hyde Park Corner

VICTORIA INN

Friendly, stucco-fronted Pimlico house with no-frills. 43 rooms.
✚ F7 ✉ 65–7 Belgrave Road, SW1 ☎ 020 7834 6721, fax 020 7931 0201, www.victoriainn.co.uk Ⓜ Victoria

LONDON
travel facts

ESSENTIAL FACTS

Britain information

- Britain and London Visitor Centre ✉ 1 Lower Regent Street, south of Piccadilly Circus, SW1 ☎ 020 7808 3864, www.visitbritain.com 🕐 Daily, opening times vary 🚇 Piccadilly Circus

London information centres

- ✉ Leicester Square, W1 ☎ 020 7437 4370, www.londontown.com 🕐 Mon–Fri 8am–midnight, Sat–Sun 10–6 🚇 Leicester Square
- ✉ Waterloo International Terminus, SE1 🕐 Daily 🚇 Waterloo

Local Centres

- For detailed information on the City of London: City of London Information Centre ✉ St. Paul's Churchyard, EC4 ☎ 020 7332 1456 🕐 Easter–end Oct daily 9.30–5; Nov–Easter Mon–Fri 9.30–5, Sat 9.30–12.30
- Greenwich Tourist Information Centre ✉ 2 Cutty Sark Gardens, Greenwich, SE10 ☎ 020 8858 6376 🕐 Daily 10–5
- Richmond Tourist Information Centre ✉ Old Town Hall, Whittaker Avenue, Richmond, Surrey ☎ 020 8940 9125 🕐 Mon–Sat 10–5 (also Sun 10.30–1.30, May–Sep)

Hotel reservations

- Visit London Booking Line: www.visitlondon.com runs a hotel booking service; credit card payment only. £5 fee. Also book in person at London Information Centre (see above) for a small fee.
- The Automobile Association (AA) publishes an annual hotel guide (available from bookshops), *The Hotel Guide*, covering the whole of Britain with a section on London. Their hotel booking service ☎ 0870 5050505 is free for its members but a database of all AA inspected hotels can be found on their website. To find out more about the AA, visit www.theaa.com

London Line

- To book rock and pop concerts, London shows and big events, call Globaltickets ☎ 0870 842 2248; www.globaltickets.com, Firstcall ☎ 020 7420 0000 or Ticketmaster ☎ 020 7344 4444 (who also provide a specialist section for sports events).

Electricity

- Standard supply is 240V.
- Motor-driven equipment needs a specific frequency; in the UK it is 50 cycles per second (kHz).

Opening hours

- Major attractions: seven days a week; some open late on Sun.
- Shops: six days a week; some open on Sun. For late-night shopping (► 72).
- Banks: Mon–Fri 9.30–5; a few remain open later or open on Sat mornings. Bureaux de change generally have longer opening hours (including weekends).
- Post offices: usually Mon–Fri 9–5.30, Sat 9–12.30.

Places of worship

- Almost every denomination is represented. Refer to the Yellow Pages telephone directory.

Public holidays

- 1 Jan; Good Friday; Easter Mon; May Day (first Mon in May); last Mon in May; last Mon in Aug; 25 Dec; 26 Dec.
- Almost all attractions and shops close Christmas Day; many close 24 Dec, 1 Jan and Good Fri as well. Shops, restaurants and attractions remain open on other holidays but it is advisable to check in advance.

Student travellers

- Holders of an International Student Identity Card will be able to obtain some concessions on travel and entrance fees.

Tipping

- 10 per cent for restaurants, taxis, hairdressers and other services. Look over restaurant bills to see if service charge has already been added or is included.
- No tipping in theatres, cinemas, concert halls or in pubs and bars (unless there is waitress service).

GETTING AROUND

London Transport travel information centres

- Centres sell travel passes and provide underground and train maps, bus route maps and information on cheap tickets.
- ⊙ Daily at each terminal at Heathrow Airport and at the following stations:
  Ⓗ Hammersmith, Oxford Circus (except Sun) Piccadilly Circus, St. James's Park (except Sun), and Heathrow Terminals 1, 2 and 3
  Ⓡ Victoria, Euston, King's Cross, Paddington
- London Transport enquiries telephone service ☎ 020 7222 1234 (⊙ 24 hours).

Travel Passes

- Travelcards: valid after 9.30am (pay a surcharge to use earlier) for unlimited travel by Underground, railway, Docklands Light Railway and most buses; sold at travel information centres, British Rail stations, all Underground stations, and some shops, cover travel for one day, a week, a weekend, a month or a year. Adults need a photocard (except for a one-day travelcard), sold at travel information centres; children aged 5–15 pay child fares but need a

child-rate photocard; children under five travel free.
- Bus passes: bus-only passes are on sale at travel information centres, Underground stations and some newspaper shops.
- Visitor travelcards: similar to travelcards but no need for a photo; valid for one, three, four or seven days. Must be bought before arrival in London.
- Carnet: a book of 10 tickets for Zone 1 only.

London Pass

- This is a pass to over 50 top attractions as well as an option to travel on buses, tubes and trains. The aim of the pass is to enable you to beat the crowds lining up at selected major attractions. The pass is valid for either one, two three or six days—multi-day passes must be used on consecutive days. It offers discounts on restaurants and leisure activities. Check outwww.londonpass.com for further information.

The Tube (formerly known as the Underground)

- Twelve colour-coded lines link almost 300 stations. Use a travel pass or buy a ticket from a machine (some give change) or ticket booth; keep the ticket until the end of the journey. The system includes the Docklands Light Railway (DLR).

Buses

- Plan your journey using the latest copy of the *Central London* bus guide available at travel centres. For further information ☎ 020 7222 1234; www.thetube.com
- Children's fares are as for travel passes (see above).
- A bus stop is indicated by a red

sign on a metal pole.

- On a two-man bus, the conductor comes to inspect the travel pass or sell a ticket; on a one-man bus, the driver inspects passes or sells tickets as passengers board—try to have the exact change.

Taxis

- Drivers of official (mostly black) cabs know the city well. They are obliged to follow the shortest route unless an alternative is agreed. A black cab is licensed for up to five passengers.
- Meter charges increase in the evenings and at weekends.
- Avoid minicabs; they may have no meter and inadequate insurance.
- Black cabs can be ordered by phone: Radio Taxis ☎ 020 7272 0272

MEDIA & COMMUNICATIONS

Newspapers & magazines

- Quality papers include *The Times*, the *Financial Times*, the *Daily Telegraph*, the *Independent*, the *Guardian* and the *Sunday Times*, *Sunday Telegraph*, *Observer* and *Independent on Sunday*.
- London's only evening paper, the *Evening Standard* (Mon–Fri), first edition out around noon, is strong on entertainment and nightlife.
- *Time Out* (published weekly Wed) lists almost everything going.

Sending a letter or a postcard

- Stamps are sold at post offices and some newsagents and shops.
- Trafalgar Square Post Office stays open till late: ✉ William IV Street, WC2 🕐 Mon–Sat 8–8
- Letter boxes are red.

Telephones

- Check the mark-up rate before making a call from a hotel.

- London numbers (now 8 digits) are prefixed with the code 020 when dialing from outside the city.
- Use coins or a British Telecom (BT) phonecard to call from BT phone booths. Phonecards are sold at post offices and newsagents. Many phones take credit cards.
- Information ☎ 192
- Operator ☎ 100 to check costs, reverse charges, or call another person in the UK via the operator.
- Directory enquiries: ☎ 118 118
- International telephoning: ☎ 153 for directory enquiries; ☎ 155 to reverse charges.
- To call the US from the UK dial the code 001.
- Beware of high charges on some premium rate numbers (prefixed 09) and special rate (08) numbers.

Television

- BBC 1 (varied); BBC 2 (more cultural); ITV (commercial—varied); Channel 4 (commercial—cultural and minority interest); Channel 5 (commercial—varied); satellite and cable channels (mainly in larger hotels) include CNN, MTV and Sky. A few provide digital TV.

EMERGENCIES

Emergency telephone numbers

- For police, fire or ambulance, ☎ 999 from any telephone, free of charge. The call goes directly to the emergency services. Tell the operator which street you are on and the nearest landmark, intersection or house number; stay by the telephone until help arrives.

Embassies

- Australian High Commission ✉ Australia House, Strand, WC2 ☎ 020 7379 4334

- Canadian High Commission ✉ 38 Grosvenor Street, W1 ☎ 020 7258 6600
- New Zealand High Commission ✉ New Zealand House, 80 Haymarket, SW1 ☎ 020 7930 8422
- Embassy of the United States of America ✉ 24 Grosvenor Square, W1 ☎ 020 7499 9000

Lost credit cards

- Report any loss immediately to the relevant company and to the police also call your bank.
- To discover your credit card company's local 24-hour emergency number ☎ 192 (information).

Medical treatment

- EU nationals and citizens of some other countries with special arrangements (Australia and New Zealand) may receive free National Health Service (NHS) medical treatment. All other visitors, including those from the US, have to pay.
- If you need an ambulance ☎ 999 on any telephone, free of charge.
- NHS hospitals with 24-hour emergency departments include: University College Hospital ✉ Gower Street (entrance in Grafton Way), WC1 ☎ 020 7387 9300; Chelsea and Westminster Hospital ✉ 369 Fulham Road, SW10 ☎ 020 8746 8000
- Private hospitals, with no emergency unit, include the Cromwell Hospital ✉ Cromwell Road, SW5 ☎ 020 7460 2000
- Great Chapel Street Medical Centre ✉ 13 Great Chapel Street, W1 ☎ 020 7437 9360 is an NHS clinic open to all, but visitors from countries without the NHS reciprocal agreement must pay.
- Dental specialist: contact British Dental Association ☎ 020 7935 0875. Helpline 0870 3331188

- Eye specialist: Moorfields Eye Hospital ✉ City Road, EC1 ☎ 020 7253 3411; Dolland & Aitchison ✉ 229–31 Regent Street, W1 ☎ 020 7499 8777 (opticians and on-site workshop for glasses and contact lenses).
- For homeopathic pharmacies, practitioners and advice: the British Homeopathic Association ✉ 27a Devonshire Street, W1 ☎ 020 7566 7800

Medicines

- Many drugs cannot be bought over the counter. For an NHS prescription, pay a modest flat rate; if a private doctor prescribes, you pay the full cost. To claim charges back on insurance, keep receipts.
- Chemists open late include: Bliss Chemist ✉ 5 Marble Arch, W1 ☎ 020 7723 6116 🕔 Daily 9am–midnight
- Ainsworth's Homeopathic Pharmacy ✉ 38 New Cavendish Street ☎ 020 7935 5330 🕔 Mon–Fri 9–5.30, Sat 9–4

Sensible precautions

- Do not wear valuables that can be snatched. Valuables should be kept in a hotel or bank safe box.
- Make a note of all passport, ticket and credit card numbers, and keep it in a separate place.
- Keep money, passport and credit cards in a fully closed bag. Carry only a small amount of cash and keep it out of sight.
- Keep your bag in sight at all times —do not sling it over your back or put it on the floor of a café, pub or cinema.
- At night, try not to travel alone; if you must, either pre-book a taxi or keep to well-lit streets and use a bus or underground train where there are already other people.

Index

CityPack
London *Top 25*

ABOUT THE AUTHOR
Louise Nicholson has lived in Islington, in central London, since 1976, working as a freelance writer and
campaigning for the conservation of buildings. She is the author of several books about London, including
Fodor's London Companion, *National Geographic Traveler London* and *Look Out London!*, a guide for children.
She also travels widely and has written a number of guide-books to India.

WRITTEN BY AND EDITION REVISER Louise Nicholson
CONTRIBUTIONS TO LIVING LONDON Paul Wade and Kathy Arnold
UPDATED BY   Apostrophe S Limited
COVER DESIGN   Tigist Getachew and Fabrizio La Rocca

A CIP catalogue record for this book is available from the British Library.

ISBN-10: 0 7495 4014 1
ISBN-13: 978 0 7495 4014 2

The contents of this publication are believed correct at the time of printing. Nevertheless, the publishers cannot
be held responsible for any errors or omissions or for changes in the details given in this guide or for the
consequences of any reliance on the information provided by the same. This does not affect your statutory
rights. Assessments of attractions, hotels, restaurants and so forth are based upon the author's own personal
experience and, therefore, descriptions given in this guide necessarily contain an element of subjective opinion
which may not reflect the publishers' opinion or dictate a reader's own experiences on another occasion. We
have tried to ensure accuracy in this guide, but things do change and we would be grateful if readers would
advise us of any inaccuracies they may encounter.

Published by AA Publishing (a trading name of Automobile Association Developments Limited, whose
registered office is Southwood East, Apollo Rise, Farnborough, Hampshire GU14 0JW.
Registered number 1878835).

© **AUTOMOBILE ASSOCIATION DEVELOPMENTS LIMITED 1996, 1997, 1999, 2002, 2004, 2005**
First published 1996. Reprinted Jan, Mar, Oct, Dec 1998, Mar 1999
Revised second edition 1997. Reprinted Mar 1998
Revised third edition 1999. Revised fourth edition 2002; Reprinted May 2002. Reprinted Jan 2003. Revised fifth
edition 2004. Reprinted May 2004. Information verified and updated 2005.

Colour separation by Keenes, Andover
Printed and bound by Hang Tai D&P Limited, Hong Kong

ACKNOWLEDGEMENTS
The Automobile Association would like to thank the following photographers, libraries and associations for their
assistance in the preparation of this book.
BRIDGEMAN ART LBRARY, LONDON 16l The Tower of London, from a survey made in 1597 by W. Haiward and
J Gascoyne (engraving) by English School (19th century) Stapleton Collection, UK, 16/17 Great Fire of London,
1666 by Lieve Verschuier (1630-86) Museum of Fine Arts, Budapest, Hungary; © BRITISH MUSEUM 45;
HULTON GETTY 17l, 17r; NATIONAL PORTRAIT GALLERY 40t, 40b; PICTOR INTERNATIONAL, LONDON 24r;
ROBERT HARDING PICTURE LIBRARY 14l, 14c, 19tl, 24l, 60; SCIENCE MUSEUM 29; SPECTRUM COLOUR
LIBRARY 31, 34; STOCKBYTE 5.
The remaining photographs are held in the Association's own library (AA PHOTO LIBRARY) and were taken by
MAX JOURDAN with the exception of the following:
PETER BAKER cover: Tower Bridge; CAROLINE JONES 21; PAUL KENWARD 20tc, 22tr; S & O MATHEWS cover:
St Paul's Cathedral; 48b; JENNY MCMILLAN 24tr; JOHN MILLER 7; ROBERT MORT cover: telephone box, 20r,
50b; BARRIE SMITH cover: Westminster Abbey, man at antique market, 26t, 26b, 27, 32b, 37t, 42t; RICK
STRANGE cover: Underground sign, Royal Albert Hall, 21tc, 28t, 28b, 30t, 30b, 32t, 48t, 49, 51t, 52, 62; JAMES A
TIMS cover: taxi, 23tl; MARTIN TRELAWNY 21tl, 23tc, 44t, 58; ROY VICTOR cover: guard, 25t; PETER WILSON 41,
46b, 55; TIM WOODCOCK 35t, 36, 39b, 46t, 57; WYN VOYSEY 6tr, 35b, 37b, 38, 42b, 50t, 59; CLIVE SAWYER 56.

A02290
Maps © Automobile Association Developments Limited 1996, 1999, 2002, 2004, 2005

OS Ordnance
    Survey®

This product includes mapping data licensed from Ordnance Survey® with the
permission of the Controller of Her Majesty's Stationery Office. © Crown copyright
2005. All rights reserved. Licence number 399221

Fold-out map © MAIRDUMONT / Falk Verlag 2005
Transport map TCS, Aldershot, England

TITLES IN THE CITYPACK SERIES
• Amsterdam • Bangkok • Barcelona • Beijing • Berlin • Boston • Brussels & Bruges •
• Chicago • Dublin • Florence • Hong Kong • Lisbon • Ljubljana • London • Los Angeles •
• Madrid • Melbourne • Miami • Milan • Montréal • Munich • Naples • New York • Paris •
• Prague • Rome • San Francisco • Seattle • Shanghai • Singapore • Sydney • Tokyo •
• Toronto • Venice • Vienna • Washington, D.C. •